Crossover City

Crossover City

Resources for Urban Mission
and Transformation

Edited by
Andrew Davey

mowbray

Published by Mowbray, a Continuum imprint
The Tower Building, 11 York Road, London SE1 7NX
80 Maiden Lane, Suite 704, New York NY 10038

www.continuumbooks.com

First published 2010.

British Library Cataloguing-in-Publication Data
A catalogue record for this book is available from the British Library.

ISBN 978-1-4411-3864-4

Typeset by Kenneth Burnley, Wirral, Cheshire
Printed and bound by MPG Books Ltd, Bodmin, Cornwall

Contents

Part 5: Engaging: Four Case Studies

Foreword

I was leading the debate when the Church of England report, *Faithful Cities*, was discussed at the July 2006 sessions of the General Synod. When an amendment was tabled to 'ask the Mission and Public Affairs Council to convene a group to provide additional input on the theology and practice of urban mission', I was very pleased to welcome the proposal, and the motion was duly amended by Synod.

This book is the result of that work. An Urban Theology and Mission Group was commissioned with the task, chaired by Bishop Laurie Green. It has explored and engaged with a spectrum of approaches and expectations in urban mission. I think you will find here new light shed upon the tensions of urban ministry and mission, as well as fresh insights into familiar questions. A particular benefit has been the breadth of approach, and the depth of listening apparent among those who have participated in this process. The participants themselves claim to have been changed by the process in which they have been engaged, and they share their journey with us.

St Paul tells us in his letter to the urban Philippians that our 'citizenship' (πολίτευμα) is in heaven. By this he does not mean that belonging to a worldly community, be it urban, rural or suburban, is of little significance, because our main focus is on the hereafter. On the contrary, he is saying that we have a choice as to what kind of society we build. A society built on the pursuit of selfish desire, on greed and on degrading the glory of God in humanity made in his image, focuses its citizenship, its 'conversation' (Authorized Version) – perhaps we would say 'dialogue' – somewhere else entirely. With the hellish mess we have too often made of our urban social landscape, the paralysis we have experienced as regeneration schemes come and go leaving many problems unchanged, and the dangerous disenchantment and hopelessness of many of our young people, we need to recover a sense not only of what citizenship should consist of, but also where its focus should be. As Christians we have to raise our sights – human beings are to reflect God's glory, and it is for us, corporately, to make Christ visible. Our active citizenship must be to aim for the highest, the best, and the way that is truest to our very high calling, and to do it for everyone, especially for the poor.

Crossover City does just this – it raises our sights, and it will raise the game for many of those engaged with passion and delight in the joys and struggles of urban ministry. This ministry is lived out in the shadow of the cross and in the light of the resurrection. It is a ministry of pain and healing, of suffering and joy. Increasingly it is a complicated ministry, as communities within communities learn to live creatively with difference and diversity, and to celebrate these as gracious gifts of God. Our deliberations in urban theology, reflected in the various essays in this book, are all geared to helping God's people in the city live out the joy, simplicity and compassion of the gospel.

This book should go some way, or so I hope and pray, to open the ears of some of our clergy to the call of God to the inner city, and to ministry on 'difficult' estates. It is here, as much as anywhere else, that so often God surprises us with his Bethel: 'How awesome is this place! This is none other than the house of God. This is the gate of heaven' (Genesis 28.17).

+ Sentamu Ebor

Introduction:
Deep Theology for a Spacious City?

The Church is in the city. From its earliest days Christianity has been concerned with mission in and to urban places. Christians have gathered across urban communities celebrating their common life as they intercede for the *polis* for which that life offers a model. Hospitality has been offered, the hungry have been fed and hope has been offered. Cities have celebrated faith through their built environment, in street-level celebrations and civic discourse, but have also been places where the image of God has been desecrated through poverty, exclusion and violence.

Through its many presences and interventions, the Church has taken part in what has become known as 'urban mission', sharing in the mission of God in a defined social and geographical context, through institutions, religious orders, settlements and new forms of Church, as well as in the daily round of good neighbourliness, prayer and participation in community life. Through practice theology has happened, occasionally being committed to the written and printed page, offering glimpses of faithfulness, transformation and new possibilities.

The late twentieth century and early twenty-first century have seen significant changes in our towns and cities through de-industrialization, economic restructuring, regeneration and migration. Many of these changes have been documented by reports such as *Faith in the City*, *Faithful Cities* and the Methodist *Cities* report. Those changes have presented challenges concerning the unequal distribution of wealth and opportunity, as well as the programmes and partnerships in which the Church participates.

The Church has also been changing as new styles of urban mission have emerged as different groups have caught a vision of God's kingdom at work and brought new energy and questions with them. Mission and evangelism are core activities for Christians in urban areas, but models and agendas which become normative are often formed in very different communities. Theology is disentwined from place, often in danger of serving other masters. The Church can at times mirror or acquiesce with that inequality that is found deeply entrenched.

In 2006 the Urban Mission and Theology Group received the mandate 'to provide additional input on the theology and practice of urban mission' following the *Faithful Cities* report. Though the starting point for the group's thinking and a number of these essays is the *Faithful Cities* report, *Crossover City* is not a reflection on that report and its theology, or an assessment of the impact of its recommendations, but an attempt to ask how we might meaningfully speak of and practise urban mission at the beginning of the twenty-first century. In the group's work there has been an attentiveness to the shifts that have taken place across the presences we find among urban churches. We were aware of the urgent need for reflection on how church planting and discipling happen among those who are often the focus rather than the initiators of 'project work'.

Crossover City attempts to return to theological and missiological foundations by examining some of the essential categories through which the Church reflects on its mission and its distinctiveness. The authors, drawn from a range of theological backgrounds, have attempted to confront the theological priorities of the Church as it attempts to hold the tensions between expectations of its partnership in social regeneration and welfare, and its prophetic voice through its continued and transformative presence in the poorest marginalized communities. They have also been aware of the need to consider the many communities over which the 'urban fabric' stretches, conscious that urban mission needs to be an issue for suburban, ex-urban and city centre Christians. The flourishing of a predominantly urban society is about the welfare and involvement of the whole of this population, including many who choose to live in rural areas yet shape the lives of our cities in their working lives. As many people participate in the life of increasingly interdependent and complex urban communities, they need to hear the invitation of Dorren Massey to engage in 'the possibility of thinking of placed identity not as a claim *to* a place but as the acknowledgement of the responsibilities that inhere in *being placed*' (Massey, 2007: 216). Those responsibilities may be practised in the tenants' hall or at the school gate, in the city hall or boardroom of a company with links to cities across the globe. They are also performed by the Church as it inhabits its place – maybe consciously as a *parish* church, but also in an identification with a neighbourhood or the range of flows that connect the lives of its members with different parts of the city and urban places on other continents.

At times we have been aware of greater competitiveness and separation among expanding congregations, of fragmentation and contestation between groups in marginal decline, as well as those who have yet to find their sure footing. There has been a determination to counter the way theology is often done by isolated factions that deny the openness and collaboration which must underpin the transformative mission that our urban areas cry out for. This is why the issues addressed include contested areas often approached as touchstones of association for some groups. *Crossover City* sets out to interrogate our current practice and vocabulary of urban mission, asking: How is urban mission understood in terms of evangelism and proclamation? What are the prophetic or missional consequences of a moral account of urban life? How does the urban affect one's understanding of sin and salvation, the work of the sacraments and the Holy Spirit; and the challenge of Christ in the lives of his followers?

First, Laurie Green and Jon Kuhrt reflect on the contested arena of urban theological practice. Reflecting on the process through which this book came about, they identify the fears and suspicions of a call to urban ministry faced by many who fear the hybridity and unpredictability such a call might carry. Green considers the nature of the urban vocation and explores how the testimony of many is that to answer such a call leads to a discovery of the authenticity of theology in conversation and negotiation that acknowledges the shifts taking place in the crossovers found in the Church's urban presence. Kuhrt considers how urban theological practice will demand a sensitivity to their range of approaches and practices while resisting tribal–silo-based theologies that consume time and resources.

Andrew Davey considers the particularities of the urban and the rapidity of change that is increasingly acknowledged. The significance of the network, of spatial reordering and connectivity interact with notions of neighbourhood, place and, for Anglicans at least, 'the parish'. The multidirectional nature of urban mission and social transformation is underlined.

Over two chapters Peter Robinson reconsiders two areas of missional practice, preaching and evangelism. He reflects on approaches to proclamation through preaching, drawing on the themes of resistance, contextualization, learning, discovery and solidarity. For Robinson, preaching is closely tied with the articulation of 'little theologies' and the struggle to make places 'more human'.

Mandy Ford and Jon Kuhrt consider the language of sin and salvation and the theological resources needed to renegotiate a critical area of theological discourse. Urban communities are often perceived pessimistically; there is so much that seems wrong in the lives of urban people, but are they actually sinful places? Personal and structural transformation is about relationship, with God and with each other, as well as our complicity in the failure to resist sin. Faith and action combine in God's economy, offering a foretaste of the age to come.

Andrew Davey considers the Christological dimension through which an urban church finds itself engaging with dense presence of Christ in the downtrodden, the coming kingdom, scapegoat nailed to the cross, and in the dynamic of his body that is the Church. Mandy Ford considers a sacramental theme from the perspective of urban church culinary practice. How does the Eucharist connect with the 'long chain of meals', which are characteristic of urban church life? Ford considers the hospitality and companionship offered in the radical commensality of the 'bring and share' to offer a new reading of the Eucharistic feast.

Laurie Green considers the life of the Spirit within the creativity and boundary crossing we find in urban life. Rather than shunning the material, the Spirit enables us to engage with the physicality of the city, calling for a new theology of the inhabitation of space with spiritual presence.

While drawing on the experience and practice of the writing group, we were constantly reminded of many ways in which urban theological practice is grounded in towns and cities today. Our case studies offer portraits of how urban engagement and church life is challenging and changing those called to be disciples in the city. Honesty and faithfulness begin to mark four particular paths of congregations and their leaders as they explore the deep presence of the divine call.

Acknowledgements

As editor and convenor I am indebted to members of the Urban Mission and Theology Group for their energy, support and writing over the past three years. We are grateful to the Mission and Public Affairs Council of the Archbishops' Council for support and resources for the group's meeting. While the work of the group follows a request from the Council, the final form and content of the project is the responsibility of the Urban Mission and Theology Group, and a reflection of the inter- action and goading we shared together.

Contributors

Mandy Ford is Vicar of Christ the King, Beaumont Leys in Leicester and Diocesan Church Urban Fund Link Officer. She is currently undertaking doctoral studies at Nottingham University.

Peter Robinson is Archdeacon of Lindisfarne, in the Diocese of Newcastle. He was previously Director of the Urban Ministry and Theology Project, and Priest in Charge, St Martin's Byker, Newcastle. Peter chairs the William Temple Foundation.

Andrew Davey is National Adviser on Community and Urban Affairs for the Church of England. He lives in inner London, where he has been a parish priest. He is author of *Urban Christianity and Global Order* and *The Urban Challenge*.

Jon Kuhrt is Director of Community Mission, Livability (previously Shaftesbury Society). Jon co-authored *Just People?*, a six-week course for churches on compassion and social justice. Before joining Shaftesbury in 2002, Jon managed hostels for homeless young people for the charity Centrepoint in Soho, London.

Laurie Green is Bishop of Bradwell, having previously been a parish priest in Birmingham and London, and Principal of the Aston Training Scheme. His books include *Let's Do Theology* (revised 2009), *The Impact of the Global*; and *Urban Ministry and the Kingdom of God*.

David Nixon is Rector of Stoke Damerel and St Aubyn, Devonport in Plymouth. His doctoral thesis concerned a theology of homelessness. He is currently an honorary research fellow in the University of Exeter.

Anna Thompson is Eden Network National Development Co-ordinator for The Message Trust and lives in Openshaw, east Manchester.

Tom Gillum is Warden of the Community of St Jude, Earl's Court, London.

Part 1

Calling and Crossover

Chapter 1

'I Can't Go *There!*': The Urban Vocation

LAURIE GREEN

One of the responsibilities of the bishop is to engage with parishes in need of a parish priest and to encourage an appropriate deployment so that both needy and prosperous parishes are fully staffed. However, of late there has been a new reluctance on the part of ordained ministers to opt for the more sacrificial ministries such as those in deprived urban locations. Prosperous parishes certainly can present real challenges in ministry, but there is something about urban deprivation which alarms many priests and drives them to look elsewhere. My suspicion is that the reasons for this are not as simple as they first appear. To begin with, there is of course the obvious challenge of living in a deprived area with the lack of social infrastructure, health care, shops, open space and amenities. Many a priest will say to me, 'I cannot in all conscience visit that deprivation upon my family.' My usual rejoinder is to say, 'Can you not see what cultural deprivation you may be introducing your family to if you live in a monocultural, well-heeled parish where no one has a clue about the issues which others face?' But my impassioned plea is not given much credence.

But when I dig deeper I sense that this reluctance to minister in tough urban areas is not born simply from a personal quest for an easier life – there are other more subtle fears at work. For example, many of our newer ordinands have served already in a professional capacity in industry or commerce and have therefore become steeped in a culture where success, measurable achievement targets and status are the criteria by which one's working life might be judged. In the deprived urban areas all these things are rarely considered of consequence and are unlikely to be the pay-off of hard work and commitment. To work in a parish where some, including some church structures, are always by these criteria going to assume you to be a failure, takes courage and a depth of spiritual self-confidence.

Second, the urban scene also presents a difficult environment for the more traditional church. For while such a church expects its members to engage in rather antiquated forms of committee decision-making, to assume a dominantly middle-class, literate culture and commit free time weekly on a regular basis, the urban scene simply does not function in that way. The traditional church is expecting its members to adopt forms of interaction and worship which do not come easy to local people. To expect the clergy to inflict these alien forms on the community is to set them up for failure. If they themselves are imbued with the same churchy nineteenth-century ethos, no wonder they don't want to go to a place where they will be thought an oddity.

If, on the other hand, the candidate is up for the urban culture, then he or she faces yet another challenge and will find that, unless exceptionally lucky, the physical and financial resources available from within the congregation or offered by the wider church will be minimal. He or she will have to function on a shoe-string and may find that while local skills are abundant, they are not appropriate to running effective church councils, accounting charity finances and tackling the administration of the parish. The priest therefore has to become a generalist, taking on many tasks for which he or she has had no training, and maybe no inclination under other circumstances, to pursue.

The urban priest who yearns to be part of a local church which really engages with the community must therefore be adept at mining the particular resources which are there in the local people, digging deep to find the resources from within him- or herself, and be attuned to the powerful spiritual gifts of prayer, worship and discernment. For example, one of the great challenges which faces many a priest is the extreme urban diversity of ethnicity and culture. The urban scene – even in the social and council housing estates up and down the country – is no longer comprised of a monochrome, white, working-class culture, and the priest who seeks to engage in the realities of local people will often find in just one parish many disparate cultural silos of marginalized and deprived groups. Caribbean elderly may be fearful of the African incomers who in turn meet with only their own national group, worried about the vast numbers of the 'Asian' community that surrounds them, although that Asian community may in fact be fragmented into many religious, national and cultural segments who find their opposite numbers intimidating and alien. The British National Party may gain some members from the fearful and aggrieved of the white working class, while other white people are actually from Eastern Europe and find the local language difficult. Some of the indigenous whites may have Irish or English roots and may be happier to keep themselves to themselves. Seeking to 'build community' in such a place requires spiritual gifts of discernment and courage that elude the average minister. It calls for resources of physical stamina, warmth of personality, spiritual attentiveness and, above all, theological acuity. For when so many disparate groups offer such varying systems of meaning and value into the culture, how is one to process all that in a way that can make sense from the perspective of a Christian understanding of reality? With so many gods on offer and so many ways in which society is constructed and meanings perceived, the Christian minister must constantly be reflecting theologically at a profound level and acting out of that reflection in courageous and prophetic ways.

It is no wonder therefore that many find all this just too much of a challenge and seek ministry elsewhere in places where things are so much easier. Eddie was such a one, and shared with me when I suggested a challenging urban parish, that for him it just wasn't on: 'I simply can't go there.' It was soon afterwards that he went on a week's retreat at a Roman Catholic community house, and there in the chapel, as he was praying before a large crucifix, he recognized that the cross of our Lord Jesus makes demands upon us that defy human reckoning. He had a deep conviction that he had to say yes to the urban parish. Some years later Eddie says, 'If I had said no, I would never have encountered such joy in the gospel that has been the daily experience in my urban parish – I would never have encountered Jesus in that transforming way.' For while the cross of Jesus casts its shadow over us, laying upon us the mandate of self-sacrificial love for the least and most despised of God's children, wherever they are, so that same cross also promises resurrection joy and new life for us. As we contemplate it, it demands that we listen to the voice of the Spirit asking, 'What are you prepared to sacrifice for Jesus since he has sacrificed so much for you?', and at the same time it promises a healing and an entry into new awareness, such that we can count all the usual trappings of life – as Paul has it – as 'so much garbage' (Philippians 3.7).

To embark on this urban journey of discovery can demand great courage of those whose natural environment is not urban, but it is a journey which must be undertaken with eyes wide open. This 'journey downwards', as John Vincent calls it, is not to be undertaken in order to theologically 'gentrify' the working class (1982: 14). It is all so easy to enter into a deprived area or culture in the way some missionaries of old did – expecting to introduce God into the place of mission and in fact introducing only an alien, gentrified culture. It is altogether another matter to enter in with trepidation, taking off our shoes, as we are on 'holy ground', knowing that God is to be encountered already there with his poor. The cross demands that we enter in where God has already gone before, and the proof of God's incarnate presence already there with the marginalized is there for us all to see on the cross. We must step warily, for we may go into urban mission intent on building up and enlarging the Body of Christ, while on the cross we see Jesus giving that very body away and sacrificing it to death. So the purpose of our entering into the marginal place is not to impose our culture or to win spiritual 'market share' but to give ourselves away, to listen with rapt attention and meet Jesus there. If we boldly take up the urban vocation and venture into that new place, it will be the Spirit of Jesus who will determine the outcome of that encounter, not us.

A new theological place – 'I can't go *there!*'

So the challenge of the urban can overwhelm us so much that we just cannot face living and ministering there. We do find some parish ministers and congregations however who still manage to live in the midst of the urban but without engaging with it. For an inward-looking congregation can so easily be a silo of sanctuary from the urban world, wrapped up in its own life and sub-culture, with no time to engage or awareness of why it should be necessary to do so. They will find it odd that those around in the community simply don't seem to want to join them for church worship on Sunday mornings, and indeed even blame them for their lack of attendance and purity. What such a congregation is failing to acknowledge is that it is easy to get locked into our own membership, blinded by the togetherness of the 'in' group to what may be worthwhile and exciting outside it.

Some years ago I had such an experience but in an altogether different context. I had had profound disagreements with another member of the clergy to the point where we found it distasteful not to be in warmer communion with one another. We had been seen to disagree in the public arena on a number of theological issues – he from a more traditionalist perspective and me from a more liberal understanding. Our differences had been catalogued and were very evident, and we both held our positions with some determination and strong support from our constituencies. We felt, however, that it was not doing either of us any good spiritually to be locked in 'combat' in this way, and so we determined to meet in private for a series of conversations, in order to speak honestly and openly to one another, and seek more mutual understanding of our points of view. We met regularly for quite a time, although nobody knew that these conversations were taking place. The outcome was unexpected for both of us. After some time, we both began to enjoy one another's company more and more, savouring the interchanges that we had on each topic of disagreement, and hearing, sometimes for the first time, what it was that motivated us to think in the ways we did. We were both being opened up to new perspectives and truths, and as we recognized that, we were encouraged by the evident presence of the Holy Spirit in our midst, helping us to love one another as Christians, despite our differing opinions, even on crucial matters of belief and biblical interpretation.

At one meeting it dawned on us both simultaneously that we were now on dangerous ground, not because we were finding ourselves occasionally in agreement, but because it would be very difficult to explain to our colleagues how well we were now getting on. It was as if we were used to living in embattled trenches and we two had ventured into no-man's-land to find that the enemy was not as bad as we had anticipated. How were we now to return to our own battle lines and be welcomed back wholeheartedly? The Church through ages long has become accustomed to labels of 'churchmanship' and spirituality that are supposed to divide us, so how can we meet one another and then return to our camp and proclaim to our respective constituencies that the labels are impeding our listening and disabling our search for truth? This has certainly been the experience in the Church of England and the wider Anglican Communion, as those who have belonged to societies and groups who are antagonistic to the ordination of women as priests have found that, when they have changed their minds and espoused that ordination, they have been spurned by their former colleagues and – to put it bluntly –

lost many of their friends who now flatly refuse to acknowledge them as 'proper Christians'. It can be a lonely experience to venture forth from one's own silo of understanding to see if the enemy is in fact a friend. Little wonder then that many priests say to me that they would love to thus venture, to see what the 'other side' truly have to say, but dare not risk the loneliness and ostracism. We are imprisoned in our silos of 'churchmanship' and theological understanding, just as we can so easily be imprisoned in any culture or sub-culture in which we have grown up. Cultures are systems of meaning and value within which we find a home, and the cultures of others can seem threatening unless we spend time living within them also. We are inheritors of our cultures and, by virtue of living within them, help to build and frame them. Many cultures exist within the Church, just as many exist within the urban environment, and we get ourselves locked in and imprisoned by theological cultures, churchmanship cultures or societal cultures at our peril, for each will blind us to the truth which other cultures may be honouring. To venture out of our cultural silo is not to deny the truth of our own group or culture, but it is to be open to the possibility that God is not confined to only one human silo. For while we may argue that 'we can't go there', God seems to be prepared to cross all barriers and enter in. Jesus thus journeys repeatedly across the Sea of Galilee into the heart of the alien culture, and finds there both mission opportunity and new truths to discover.

The mixity of the city

The fear of urban ministry for many is in the thought of being dropped into a maelstrom of cultures that we find alien and unsettling. The intensity of this urban 'mixity', as we have described it, means that you have to be very short-sighted to live in its midst and not be challenged to engage it and make some sense of it.

But all that I have so far said should not in any way be read to mean that we should be accepting of all urban cultures and never question with whom we should partner. Within the mixity of the urban space we have to negotiate with canny discernment. Of late, for example, the buzz-word in urban mission has been 'partnership', and we have been enjoined to form partnerships with the moneyed – developers, regeneration entrepreneurs and the like – in order to build projects, staff our programmes, and act as agents in the delivery of government objectives. Reports have been published, *Faithful Cities* among them, which have spoken of Christian endeavour in language derived from the prevailing urban regeneration culture – we were to quantify financially the wealth of the social or religious 'capital' that we could lay on the table as we bargained with entrepreneurs for financial support for our projects. We were cajoled into competing in the market-place against one another for the benefits which would be forthcoming if we adopted the agendas set out by government and social entrepreneurs. Many who had seen this same game being played in the 1960s and 1970s warned against forgetting our own Jesus agenda in the fight to prove that we could tick the agenda boxes of others, and we were considered rather jaundiced and envious, but with the passage of time and the demise of the culture of extravagance, the theological bankruptcy of this subservience to the culture of capital has been proven. The lesson is that we must be vigilant, as we venture out from our theological silos, not to be taken in by the world's allurements. Who was it who said, 'All power co-opts, and absolute power co-opts absolutely'?

Urban space is contested space. So in the urban scene we become masters of working within that creative tension of negotiation with the Other – we sometimes, indeed often, get it wrong just as we have described – but we are constantly having to work with difference, as a vast array of people from varying cultures, social strata and backgrounds are thrown together in close proximity. The urban scene is therefore *par excellence* the place in which to learn how to venture out of our silos, be they cultural or theological (and probably both, as we have explained) in order to break down the barriers and learn the lesson of the risk of the cross and its promise of resurrection life.

The Christian, of all people, should be ready for this challenge, since we are enjoined week by week, moment by moment in our faith, to make ourselves vulnerable to the ultimate Other – the Divine. The Christian seeks to come close to the Other in prayer, worship and contemplation, risking our vulnerability – as our sinfulness is illuminated by God's holiness – and opening ourselves to the gift of eternal life through giving ourselves away. And as we seek this communion with Godhead, so it is clear from scriptural revelation that God too enjoys negotiating with us. It is not a 'done deal' but is a constant relationship of giving and taking, learning new theological interpretations, making new friends, jettisoning old animosities, and crossing over borders. There is great joy and excitement to be found in this negotiation with the Other.

Some biblical models

Before St Paul's conversion, he spent his energies in denying the right of others to engage with the Other 'outside the box' of the Jewish law and culture. After his conversion, he continued to explore the implications of his discovery that God is not always where you expect to find him. The early Christian leaders in Jerusalem were anxious that something was afoot in Antioch that did not fit within their expectations of what the Spirit of the risen Christ was expected to do. The rumour was that non-Jews – those who were entirely outside the cultural and religious silo into which Jesus had been born – were alive now with the Holy Spirit. Barnabas as a Cypriot had grown up a Jew in a Greek environment and so was well placed therefore to understand and interpret what was going on and was sent by the Jerusalem church to Antioch to investigate. He had the insight to take Paul with him – he who had already gone the first step of the journey to the Otherness of God – and together they discovered that the Spirit was not to be confined to the culture of the Jewish people, even though the whole of the revelation thus far was founded upon and had grown up within that culture. The silos were being burst asunder just as, as Matthew pictures it, the ground and foundations were shaken asunder at the crucifixion of our Lord (Matthew 27.51) and the graves of our former reluctance were thrown open wide.

Paul goes on to open his Jewish compatriots' eyes to the Gentile newcomers' experience of the Spirit of God, and later still he opens Gentile hearts to the financial plight of a needy Jewish community in Jerusalem. He forms a bridge for both communities and he himself 'crosses over' – for, having explored the boundaries of the old dispensation, he found them wanting.

Silos are containers, parameters, within which we are able to operate only under constrained conditions. Silos are places where good things are gathered, saved and looked after, but they are not open to the elements. Silos are designed to that no contamination of the content should occur, but therefore neither can any cross-fertilization or appropriate development take place within them. The limiting strictures of theological silos are well illustrated by Job's comforters as each in turn seeks to offer to the hapless Job their contained understanding of his plight. From the silo within which each has been theologically socialized and framed, they set out their interpretation of his predicament, but Job responds to each with dull pessimism. It is then revealed to Job that these notions of God that have passed before him have been far too limited – the comforters' god is just too small to encompass the horror of Job's suffering. When Yahweh himself expands Job's frame of reference so that he perceives just something of the immensity of Godhead, then the boundaries are broken, the confinement of the silos is burst open and he knows that his redeemer lives. Silos may prove good carriers of the tradition but abjectly fail at doing justice to the ineffable grandeur and freedom of the Spirit of God.

While Job finds relief in acknowledging the uncontainable grandeur of God, Jonah on the other hand wants to escape from its implications. For silos, as well as containing the tradition, are very good at limiting implications. Jonah is called by God to undertake a sacrificial missionary journey as prophet to the Ninevites – to step outside his box and take the faith into foreign territory, a task calling for boundary-crossing and personal risk. He seeks to escape back into what he knows but is eventually made by God to acknowledge the implications of his faith and to find integrity in breaking the barriers that the old traditions reinforced but which were not according to the will of his adventurous God.

Again, Jacob is reluctant to meet Esau his brother, having cheated him of his birthright, and the tension surrounding their intended reunion is palpable. Having created such animosity, Jacob is fearful of Esau and sees him as the other, the enraged protagonist, and he goes to extraordinary lengths to placate him. But when the meeting at last occurs, the two brothers look at one another face to face and they see in the other, so the text tells us, the very face of the Lord. 'I have come into your presence as into the presence of God' (Genesis 33.10). It is in breaking out of the silos of our own making and allowing the Spirit to bring engagement within contested space that we finally meet God.

In each case, God is found where we do not expect or anticipate, and the temptation to run away from that encounter with the Other is all too evident. But breaking out from the containment of preconceptions allows for new awareness of God's grace and a new freedom in the Spirit. Likewise, running away from the urban poor is running from Jesus to where I would prefer God to be found.

Crossover

One of the gifts which the mixity of urban life has brought to the world of music is the abundance of what is called 'crossover', where an artist or composer from one musical culture ventures out of their silo into another musical genre. There are many jazz, rock and pop artists who have formed new groups where the genres are intermingled and new 'fusions' developed.

Musicians have not found this easy and have been accused of being untrue to their foundational tradition. But the best fusions are not a syncretistic mishmash but an intertwining and dialogue of musical insights and styles. No longer trapped, the musicians find new ways to express the beauty and magic of their own genre within the framework of those of others. Likewise, theologians will worry that dialogue may breed mongrel faith – and syncretism in religion has always been a danger. But there is in the cross of Christ the ingredient that will enable us to come from our theological silos and enter into foreign territory, just as 'the dear Lord enters in' at his incarnation.

How do we break open our silos? Who will help us? Jesus points time and again to the marginalized, the downtrodden, the poor. When we have status, power and authority to lose, we hang on for dear life to our silos and our ring-fenced pastures, but when our lives are lived in total vulnerability, we graze where we can. The lepers of any community are not protected from their society by the cocoons of kudos, money or self-righteousness, and are therefore well placed to see society as it truly is. Those who are cushioned from society are best placed to be blind to its realities just as those who come in from outside a community are often able to see that community and judge it. It is always said that whoever it was who discovered water, it was not a fish. So when we venture into the theological preserves of another camp we can see its truths and delusions with some clarity – as long as we treat it with respectful attention and listen and observe without prejudice.

So we can say that it is therefore dangerous to formulate any theology at a distance from the poor. Indeed, denying an urban vocation, running away from the poor, is running from Jesus to where I would prefer God to be found – for time and again Jesus tells his followers that he will forever be found among those who are in most need. So it is that the cross is what stands at the very heart of this endeavour to break out and live. The risk of being as one of the lowly is the model with which our God challenges us – to live as our Lord Jesus lived, and died! The cross placards our sin to ourselves and asks, 'What will I sacrifice?' It prompts us to lay down the burden of my own tradition – the silos that contain us – and risk our body as Christ gave up his.

The cross makes us ask, 'What is truth?' Is it the adoption of a set of given formulaic pronouncements, or is it to find oneself engulfed in an atoning relationship? My plea is for the atonement of theology, and to accept St Paul's Philippian challenge to follow Christ's example – to have the mind of Christ – and give ourselves away, not grasping at mission as if it were our own, but to count our old secure silos of culture and tradition as just so much rubbish in comparison with finding God in one another.

So we seek to allow the cross to cast its shadow over all our theological endeavours, denying ourselves, risking all, and reaching out to the Other.

With the 'cross-over' all our endeavours, we can experience the resurrection life of our conjoined communities. Our urban challenges will be arenas of communion and causes of great joy.

Our theological project

This is the experience of the group behind this book – a diverse group of urban practitioners and theologians who met together to reflect from their very different perspectives upon key themes in missiology and theology within the urban scene. The group members represented a wide range of theological approaches and constituencies – the silos of theological tradition – and have come to believe through these intense dialogues that our own urban mixity has brought us much more than if we had not ventured across the divide and heard one another. We have learnt that bringing all perspectives into the conversation can be very difficult and painful, but by letting the mission of God's kingdom dominate our agenda we have found not only common ground, but delight in our different perspectives and understandings, which in turn has encouraged us to venture further. We have not always sought consensus – far from it – but we have honestly listened and learnt. We have discovered that there are significant parts of our theologies and missiologies that we rarely open to the scrutiny of others. They often are the seed bed from which many an urban report is engendered, and while those reports give rise to hot debates in the committee room, the real passion and yearning surrounding the originating experience is all the time hidden from view.

As our discussions developed, we were less able to label and 'fix' each other within specified theological silos. As our trust one for another increased, so we recognized that we were all to some extent hybrids – taking a little from this silo and from that – none of us conservative in every regard while equally none being totally radical or liberal. And as the labels fell away, we were inclined to think that the complexity of theological sub-cultures which we were trying to represent was cut across by the individual preferences and temperaments of each member. But the silos were not altogether illusory, and we owned to one another our profound differences of perception – which we hope comes through to the reader in the essays we have shared.

If this project issues in others attempting to meet across the divides, we trust that they too will share their urban stories and theologies, and our joy and delight at meeting God where we had not expected. We hope too that some readers will even be prompted to say to themselves, 'I had not thought of urban mission, but perhaps after all I *will go there!*'

Chapter 2

Going Deeper Together: Resisting Tribal Theology

JON KUHRT

The new ecumenism

Despite the high-profile disagreements between Christians in recent years, there has been a real growth in local initiatives which bring different congregations together. This 'new ecumenism' has been primarily driven by mission initiatives which have sought to serve the needs of the local community in practical and tangible ways. Through this 'community mission' varied congregations across the United Kingdom have discovered a unity in action: a common cause as one Church that is seeking to serve the local community.

One example is in Deptford, south London, where Livability have worked with many different congregations to help them come together and sign a covenant to work for the benefit of the area. The congregations involved include Pentecostal, Salvation Army, independent charismatic, Methodist, Catholic and two very different Anglican congregations. Theologically and culturally there are many differences – but a shared desire to see Jesus have an impact in their community has drawn them together.

The impetus for congregations to work together is now coming from some unlikely sources. Over the last ten years there has been a significant shift in many Pentecostal and charismatic congregations who are now emphasizing God's saving purposes for their whole area rather than simply individuals. Initiatives such as *Redeeming our Communities*,[1] *Soul in the City* (2004), Eden[2] and Street Pastors[3] epitomize this theological and missional shift in evangelical thinking and practice.

There is also a change in many 'Churches Together' groups who have developed a much more dynamic and outward focus that moves far beyond organizing joint services. One of the best examples is *Transform Newham*[4] in east London but there is also a growing number of initiatives such as *Love Southend*[5] and, local to me, *Love Streatham*. These initiatives are bringing churches together with a purpose – to increase the impact they are having in the community. And again, more often than not, it is charismatic and Pentecostal churches that are at the forefront of this new form of ecumenism. No longer can it be said that these churches are simply interested in gathering people for praise and worship on a Sunday. The landscape is changing.

This shift is encouraging because often there is a generosity that lies behind the growing unity – a willingness to acknowledge that the Church is the Body of Christ and that other traditions have strengths that we lack. This kind of 'unity in action' is not based on a theological reductionism which purely focuses on 'activism', but it does mean passionately emphasizing first those things on which we agree: that our communities are in desperate need for love, grace and an encounter with Jesus.

It seems that the growing community focus of the charismatic and Pentecostal congregations, as well as their passion and urgency, is having a galvanizing effect on the wider Church. These churches have become the powerhouse of a new unity that is breaking out around the country – a mission-shaped movement which is in deep contrast to the tired, inward-looking ecumenism of the past.

Tribal theology

However, while there are encouraging shifts for mission and unity on a local level, there remains a theological tribalism within the institutional structures of the traditional denominations. Strongholds of disunity are more entrenched within the ecclesiastical structures than they are on the ground in communities. Despite their relative strengths, both the Church of England reports *Faith in the City* (1985) and *Faithful Cities* (2006) illustrate the failure to overcome the tribal theology that undermines the Church's mission.

Faith in the City

Back in the 1980s the Church of England's *Faith in the City* report famously irked the Thatcher government of the day. The description of it as 'pure Marxist theology' by one Cabinet member secured for it something of a legendary status within the church. Perhaps too many in the Church of England have lived off the memory of these halcyon days when the established church offered a more effective opposition than the Labour Party did!

But from within the church there was some thoughtful critique of the report. John Root wrote:

> There is no greater enemy of wholesome moral debate in our society than polarisation into strongly personal, socially conservative responses; and impersonal, strongly political ones. By contrast, scripture constantly interweaves personal holiness and political responsibility. *Faith in the City* is rightly strong on the collective injustice that creates the misery of UPAs; but it seriously neglects the effect of personal sins, such as dishonesty, laziness and sexual immorality. If the Church of England is to speak more prophetically to our society, it must learn to unite the voices of collective responsibility and personal transformation. While the report is to be commended for saying unpopular things about the former, it has been too bound by ground rules of secular debate to also speak the New Testament's words of personal rebuke, repentance and re-birth. (Root 1987: 6)

John Root's words are powerful because twenty years on they are still relevant. There remains today a real need to 'unite the voices of collective responsibility and personal transformation' in the Church's role in urban mission. Our continued tendencies towards tribal theology continue to disable the prophetic voice that the Church could have in this country.

Faithful Cities

Twenty years later the Church of England established a Commission for Urban Life and Faith which produced the report *Faithful Cities* published in 2006. Through the make-up of the Commission panel, its *modus operandi* and its final report failed to engage with the changing face of Britain and especially the Church. It failed to effectively engage with the evangelical perspective and experiences in urban mission. It was dominated by a liberal agenda which, while it succeeded in challenging structural inequality and giving interesting sociological analysis, was unable to understand the commitments driving the growing evangelical agenda for an integrated approach to social action, evangelism and church growth and unity.

During 2004 I attended many of the Commission's events and at the same time I was heavily involved in the predominantly evangelical *Soul in the City* initiative that summer. It was almost as if the two initiatives were happening in a parallel universe from each other, such was the lack of connectivity between the two.[6] The Commission for Urban Life and Faith events seemed to be operating within a culture dominated by the left-hand silo on the diagram below (p. 19). While its report acknowledged some of the new initiatives and projects emerging from evangelical and charismatic churches, it failed to give any theological analysis of why these initiatives were flourishing. No sustained or effective attempt was made to cross the cultural and theological divide.

Across the church most people agree that the report *Faithful Cities* had very little impact either on society or even within the church. Part of the reason is the far less polarized political context that it was published into compared to *Faith in the City* – but this is only half the story. The other important reason is because it failed to articulate or represent what a large part of the church feel passionate about. It simply failed to speak for their work.

On the ground, *Soul in the City* was a great example of a growing missional unity, but the ecclesiastical structures of the Church of England were unable to capture a similar unity in diversity. The Commission and its report reflected the divisions within the church rather than helping to overcome them.

The effect of tribal theology

These are simply examples of the effect of tribal theology. I believe the tribalism which drives us into cultural and theological silos is deeply undermining the Church's witness in the world.

First, it leads to brittle beliefs. If we just spend time within the silo of our tradition, only talk with those who agree with us, our beliefs are not tested, toughened or deepened by honest debate with those with different perspectives. Too often we can express ourselves confidently within the silo of our particular Christian culture but are rarely tested in robust debate. This lack of assertiveness and true confidence is not just a problem for the internal well-being of the Church – it leaves us ill equipped to articulate our faith in the public square. Too often, tribalism means we appear shrill and out of touch when speaking to those beyond the Church.

Second, it turns the Church inward. So much energy in the Church is expended on criticizing fellow Christians. The silos of disunity create safe havens from which prominent leaders can criticize 'the other', winning applause at conferences and selling books. Instead of resources, time and energy being used to send people out in mission, they are expended in deconstructing the beliefs of other Christians.

Third, we simply mirror the political divisions in the world. Rather than bearing witness to the unity of transformation in Christ, the Church breaks readily into political camps with points to score and positions of influence to fight over. Too often our disunity is simply a thin religious veneer on existing social and political divisions. Instead of meaningful relationships with a focus on mission, labels such as 'liberal' or 'fundamentalist' are used, not for self-identification but as expressions of contempt in order to write off the perspectives of fellow Christians.

Fourth and most damagingly, it leads to the Church conforming to secular orthodoxy rather than biblical orthodoxy. Instead of 'uniting the voices of collective responsibility and personal responsibility' (Root 1987) in a prophetic synthesis, we follow the basic division between conservative and liberal emphases. This secular orthodoxy shapes religion and faith in its own image, rather than God's. It is a faith that takes it cues from the 'spirit of the age' (the zeitgeist) rather than God's eternal Holy Spirit. God save us from a Church that is fluent in sociological and economic analysis but cannot speak confidently of how the Holy Spirit transforms lives.

A dialectical appreciation of Christian theology

In order to overcome this tribal theology we need to appreciate the dialectical nature of Christian truth. Instead of seeing the range of emphases on key theological issues as opposing each other, we need to understand them as a dialectic that is inbuilt into the Christian faith – that truth always involves holding contrasting factors in tension.

These creative tensions abound in Christianity. At the heart of our faith is the belief that an eternal, omnipresent God incarnated himself into a specific space and time within human history. We believe that God is both transcendent, wholly other from creation – but also immanent, a God who we can know as Father. We believe in both experience of God's grace working in our lives and in a revealed truth in the Bible. We believe in both a personal encounter of Christ and the social witness that the Church is called to live out. We believe in both the truth of the incarnation of God in Christ and the atonement that he brought about through his death. To all of these aspects of theological truth, the orthodox Christian can say 'I believe'.

It is this dialectical nature of truth that is Christianity's strength in being able to engage with the real world. It is rooted in the rabbinic tradition in which Jesus' ministry was birthed – where dialectical instructions, for example to be 'wise as serpents and innocent as doves', were common.

Grappling with the dialectics such as these is central to what it means to be part of the Body of Christ. Because in every community, whether urban or not, there are Christians whose personal beliefs or tradition of Church will have different emphases than their fellow Christians. This is both the way it has always been, and surely also the way it is meant to be, as the Church displays the rich diversity of those called to follow Jesus. As Paul wrote to the divided church in Corinth, 'though all its parts are many, they form one body' (1 Corinthians 12.12).

Tribal Theology

Liberal emphasis	Theological issue	Conservative emphasis
Social	Theological emphasis	Personal
Corporate	Focus of God's concern	Individual
Structural sin	Humanity's predicament	Personal sin
Incarnation	Means of Salvation	Atonement
Synoptic gospels	Favourite Scripture	Pauline epistles
Experience	Hermeneutic	Revelation
The present 'now'	Eschatological perspective	The eternal 'not yet'
Journey of faith	How transformation happens	Conversion
The kingdom of God	Focus of discipleship	Relationship with God
Right action	Required lifestyle	Right belief
Presence	Approach to evangelism	Proclamation
Social justice	Ethical perspective	Personal morality
Society	Locus of responsibility	Individuals/families
Tolerance	Perspective to others	Distinctiveness

The diagram sets out some of the dialectics within orthodox Christianity. Many people have travelled a journey between these emphases. In my church home group which meets weekly for Bible study and discussion, the topic of social justice is continually grappled with. Some have journeyed from a conservative emphasis on personal salvation towards a more social understanding of faith. However, there are also others who have travelled in the other direction – who have questioned the more liberal emphasis they grew up in and embraced an urgency around personal faith and a conviction on truth that they found lacking previously.

The point of this model is to help us recognize the legitimacy of the range of belief within orthodox Christianity. We need to recognize the emphasis of others and commit to informed dialogue while we keep the focus outward on our mission in the world. It will be this dual commitment to unity and mission that allows us to go deeper into Christ together.

Robust and open discussion across these silos can be energizing and exciting – *if* it is the context of mission. It *can* become a dynamic exploration which appreciates the strengths of the other position even if each group continues to disagree. I saw this kind of unity emerge during the *Soul in the City* initiative in 2004 in Leytonstone where joint work between an Anglo-Catholic congregation and the neighbouring Pentecostal church really produced fruit. After two weeks of working with the local kids, they had deepened their relationship and found a unity in mission, despite the wide difference in their theology and culture. And this is the continuing experiences we see in the 'new ecumenism' discussed above.

Going deeper together

If the Church is to be effective and to make an impact in urban issues, we urgently need Christian social thinking that is prepared to break the silos between liberal and conservative. William Temple, who as much as anyone worked for Christianity's social impact, said, 'If we have to choose between making men Christian, and the social order more Christian, we have to choose the former, but there is no such antithesis' (quoted in Sainsbury and Holden 1987: 8). Temple was right – these two emphases are deeply interrelated – but he was also right in recognizing their order of dependence on each other. The gospel must transform individuals if it is to transform society.

As we consider the Church's role in the urban context, we cannot live in the past – we have to look at what God is saying to his Church in this time. And as the high tide of Christendom recedes, it exposes a harsh reality. For there are too many large, impressive religious buildings which stand as empty relics of yesteryear, like spiritual museums of a different age. They may have served well in an age of cultural Christianity, but that age is now long gone.

We have to face the reality that without purposeful evangelistic efforts, many urban congregations will continue to die. And for those denominations their ability to provide social analysis, let alone any potential political impact, will die with it. For the Church's social and political impact is derivative – ultimately it relies on people's encounter with the risen Lord Jesus and being willing to participate in communities that in some way express this belief. In order to avoid being parasitic, the institutional social endeavours within denominations need to recognize their dependence on vibrant and healthy congregations and church growth.

The dialectics set out in the diagram are rich resources for Christian thinking and engagement with the world – they are our strength – but too often they become silos of tribal entrenchment that simply mirror the conflicts in the world. The centralized and institutional elements of the traditional denominations will not survive if they continue to be enslaved into secular divisions between liberal and conservative perspectives.

If the Church is to be effective, indeed if the Church is to survive, we must go deeper. Going deeper means venturing out into the risky places, the radical places where we speak the Word of God to both institutions and individuals; where we are unashamed to both proclaim Jesus as Lord and work in his name for restoration and justice for all.

This is a place where we *will* lose friends and cause offence, just as Jesus said we would (Luke 21.12–19). But it is here where we are really following Jesus and taking up the cross he calls us to. It is a place where we truly need to depend on the Holy Spirit rather than the spirit of the age. But it is in this place, at the foot of the cross, where the Church will rediscover its role, its calling and its power to transform our broken world in Jesus' name.

Part 2

The Enterprise of Urban Mission

Chapter 3

Being Urban Matters: What is *Urban* about *Urban Mission*?

ANDREW DAVEY

Is an urban-based approach to mission still relevant in a networked global society? If so, what is particular about the urban context for the heart of God's mission?

Being urban matters. It is about who we are as well as where we live. It is about who we know, as well as the millions of city dwellers we can never hope to know. Being urban and living in a predominantly urban world shapes the way we think, the way we live and the way we relate to others. The last twenty years have seen significant restructuring taking place in cities – financial, spatial and industrial reordering, migration and social changes have altered the way we live across urban areas. While cities are seen as the engines of economic well-being, many have been excluded from the wealth and resources that have emerged. Juliet Kilpin and Stuart Murray have a sense of urgency when they write: 'Any denomination or church network that fails to grapple with the urban challenge risks obsolescence as urbanization advances' (2007: 17). Understanding urbanization is not just for those in what used to be called 'the inner city', it is critically relevant to those living in rural areas, suburbs or smaller urban communities. Neil Brenner recently wrote:

> Urbanization is, to be sure, still manifested in the continued massive expansion of cities, city-regions, and mega-city-regions, it equally entails the ongoing socio-spatial transformation of diverse, less densely agglomerated settlement spaces that are, through constantly thickening inter-urban and inter-metropolitan infrastructural networks, being even more interlinked to the major urban centres. We are witnessing, in short, nothing less than the intensification and extension of the urbanization process at all spatial sales and across the entire surface of planetary space. (Brenner 2009: 205)

There is still, however, a well-documented antipathy to urban living within the Christian tradition (see Davey 2003 or Graham and Lowe 2009). Embracing the urban involves entering into a significant dialectic of a city that can be voracious yet also the arena of incarnation and redemption. Eldin Villafañe identifies this as present in theological education:

> Unfortunately, much of theological education does not critically fit the urban scene, often choosing to ignore the city as a positive locus of God's redemptive activity. The result is an educational process and product that approaches urban ministry as a problem rather than as an opportunity to discover signs of God's reign. (Villafañe 2006: 36)

In this chapter I want to explore how being urban can shape our involvement in God's mission – within the human density of the contemporary city, across the fragmented city, and within the multiple identities we find in the global city.

Urban mission practioners remain convinced that we do need to speak of mission and theology in locational, contextual terms, and it is in the urban situation, maybe through numerical presence of the poor, that we will come close to the essence of God's activity in the world and the divine preferential option. Sociologist AbdouMalik Simone writes of the African city as the 'large intersection of bodies in need' (Simone 2004: 3). That is the daunting perception of urban places across the globe.

Within the urban throng

The challenge of proximity or propinquity is a key theme in urban writing. What does it mean to live close to those who are not family, who one cannot assume share the common ground of values, religion or ethnicity? The propinquity we find in urban living is that defining experience where we live close to those who are different – in income, social contacts or ethnicity. Through networks we develop proximity with those who are like us in both locational and virtual settings. It is in urban areas that networks are the densest. Network can, however, exclude and allow members to opt out of locational responsibilities.

Some perceive an apparent divide in urban faith communities between

those that are location and community based, and those that are networked and eclectic. It does not necessarily follow that the latter will have
less commitment to ministries involving social justice; the nature of the
congregation may itself provide access to levels of engagement and power
which would not be possible from a smaller, community-focused congregation. How congregations are enabled to understand their impact and
profile in the place they worship in is critical. More gathered congregations can find their demographics and concerns to be out of step with the
communities on their doorstep.

In cities we live in fractured communities, in places which often seem
more the victims of exterior forces than the initiators of change. Poverty
and 'posherty' are neighbours. Wealth and poverty may rub shoulders on
the same street or in adjoining neighbourhoods. Cities are usually places
of demographic change and movement. Populations can change in less
than a generation as waves of migration come and go. Elsewhere spatial,
social and political changes can shift populations through relocation and
regeneration schemes as the built environment is renewed or areas are
gentrified. Cities are rarely benign territory; in the urban community we
discover great levels of poverty and powerlessness – people, and whole
communities, can get 'stuck' with little opportunity or access to
resources that could improve their situation. Many will be urban from
birth, part of communities based around employment, language or ethnicity, aware of the city changing near or around them and who feel
marginalized or forgotten within a familiar neighbourhood.

Others will see the urban in terms of the exotic, exciting, exceptional
or elite; in terms of culture, opportunity or experience, urban living provides opportunities as well as challenges and threats. For some, it is the
opportunity to embrace anonymity – to be part of something big and
happening without responsibilities and ties; for others, it is about new
opportunities and possibilities, maybe in work and education, to
develop their personal potential. The reality is often different from the
expectations.

Across the city we will find very dissimilar communities accessing the
same municipal services, driving or walking the same streets, sharing the
same pollution; people from social housing, older town cores and residential suburbs using the same gyms, schools, police services, voting in
the same elections – with very different experiences at times. Discover-
ing the power of agency can be a critical step in individual and commu-

nity transformation – this can come through neighbourhood action, community organizing across a borough or city. It may also come through the acknowledgement of responsibility as individuals, organizations or authorities analyse their role and influence in the forces that affect a whole municipality and beyond.

The responsibilities of place

In a fractured city we find a fractured Church uncertain how its urban, suburban, estate or city-centre presences connect. Giles Goddard suggests that each 'person starts from a place that is both broken and redeemed' (Goddard 2008: 85). I suspect when we look at the Church across a city we are aware of that tension and the need not just to discover faithfulness but also to enable broken connections with neighbourhood and the wider city community to be rebuilt. Each place, and networked node, has potential as an arena for the activities of redemption. The linkage between suburban and urban parishes must be more than just a grudgingly shared common purse or a paternalistic twinning arrangement. Albert Hsu quotes Gaylord Noyce: 'The suburban congregation has a moral responsibility to the life of the entire metropolis' (Hsu 2006: 177) as they seek a larger vision for God's transformational work that reaches beyond private elite living space (Hsu: 53). Urban geographer Doreen Massey has recently written of 'the possibility of thinking of placed identity not as a claim *to* a place but as the acknowledgement of the responsibilities that inhere in *being placed*' (Massey 2007: 216).

Together with this we find many who spend their professional lives shaping the city withdrawing at the end of the day across the city boundaries to suburbanized commuter villages (this can have consequences for the financial base of the city as well as the Church's understanding of its integrity). The notion of the city-region has an important role to play in reshaping the imagination of the connections (and responsibilities) between places that people inhabit and work. Elsewhere gentrification displaces older populations or creates pockets of deprivation (usually social housing) within areas of wealth where house and service prices escalate. Such new populations rarely invest in the local: their presence can lead to decline in local services and other tensions. The Church needs to be aware of how urban space is contested and the inherent issues of social justice, engaging alongside others to seek justice in housing and community life (see Slater 2009).

Urban mission needs to take into account the temporal as well as the power dimensions of the city's shifting population. The intervention on a weekday lunchtime in a financial district can provide the critical opportunity for significant issues of faith and practice to be raised which might not be so directly addressed in a suburban or eclectic Sunday service. A presence within the night-time economy of the city centre finds another temporal layer of spiritual need in a community at other times dispersed.

Urban mission is not about taking advantage of 'the opportunities' because of the levels of poverty or disorientation we find in the urban community. Missional transformation seeks to bring about change from as near as possible to those for whom that change is good news, enabling them to experience and become agents of transformation. From the apostolic mission onwards the Church has been in the midst of rapidly changing urban culture. At times it has been indistinguishable from the ruling urban hegemonies, at other times it has offered an alternative city. In 1991 Aylward Shorter wrote of 'the Christian task in Africa [being] the evangelization of a continent in the process of rapid urbanization [and] to a great extent, the evangelization of the urbanization process itself'. Shorter concludes that the accomplishment of the Christian response will be how those processes become 'less invidious and less unjust, more human, more enduringly creative' (Shorter 1991: 148).

How do we engage with the mission of God in the city as a social reality, albeit one whose future is unspecified? It is not so much a case of accepting the city – warts and all – but learning to live that vibrant, kaleidoscopic urbanity ('thrown togetherness') in the pursuit of the kingdom and human flourishing for the children of God. We need to understand the nature of social struggles in their local and extended place, as well as the struggles for space, physical and cultural. As Christians we may need to be developing a malleable missiological vocabulary that captures 'the changing cartography of our cities' – this is a mission field that does not stand still to be 'photographed, analysed and measured' (see Keith 2003: 3).

Global place

As some of the voices we have already heard remind us, urban mission has a global dimension. We are constantly reminded that our world balance has shifted. The majority of the global population now live in urban areas. A sizeable part of that majority will not live in the towers of concrete and steel but in slums, holding on to the fringes of settlements, on the edges of polluted rivers and rubbish tips. Urban settlements are expanding into city regions as ex-urban and suburban communities join conurbations at the edges. The process has a range of impacts in different continents – but these are rarely unconnected. Urban geographers have mapped some of those interdependencies and impacts, but also the responsibilities of being in critical places which are the connections and nodes. Global flows and processes are not planned but are often the cause of an imbalance of economic power. Those with least power may also be those who we find in the burgeoning cities of the global South or on the move between those cities and those in Europe and north America. As in previous centuries the mission will be present within such global flows in surprising, often counter-cultural and at times corrupted forms.

The recent jubilee debt and trade justice campaigns, and now the climate change initiative have enabled people to grapple with issues of injustice within global economic flows, and their own complicity within 'the system'. Partnership arrangements between different locations within the global Church need to take seriously how cities have direct competitive and asymmetrical relationships:

> Any theory of urban justice must wrestle with the extent to which a just arrangement for those within one's city's borders could coexist with, or depend upon, unequal or exploitative relations with inhabitants of other cities and non-urban areas. (Connolly and Steil 2009: 6)

Missional transformation involves responding to the call to model and centre our lives, collective and individual, on the kingdom of God, and to seek justice and welfare, to include the marginal, strengthen the weak and to challenge the practice and structures of sin that is the abuse and misuse of God-given lives. Urban mission calls people to participate in the life of kingdom in a particular context 'speaking a certain language, telling a certain story, witnessing to certain non-negotiable things about humanity and about the context in which humanity lives' (Williams 2002). As David Ford writes:

> Mutual responsibility with compassion and free, respectful communication can be rooted in a created and redeemed sociality which is not just seen as the right moral answer to city problems but as good news whose very recognition and celebration allows it to be realised further. (Ford 1989: 255)

This cannot be solely an individual acquisition of faith but a shared discovery of place and community, of life 'in Christ' looking towards and living a new urban order.

Being urban

Put 'urban' into a search engine on the internet and you will find a profusion of sites dedicated to black music and culture. Hip-hop, street dance, R&B are all part of an astute urban-based culture with roots in the segregated cultures of American cities.

Engaging with the urban expressive culture will take us into places where there is suspicion of or complete alienation from the multitude of programmes, bodies, boards and partnerships concerned with the regeneration and renewal of our urban areas. Robert Beckford has been an often lone voice writing of the difficulties getting black urban churches to connect with this gritty urbanism they find around them and within the cultures that their young people inhabit. Many factors contribute to a failure to grasp or engage with the alienation of a black generation, its manifestations and discover possibilities for transformation. Beckford identifies a reluctance to analyse churches' social location or to allow theology to enter into dialogue with contemporary black urban culture and analytical frameworks, leaving attempts at mission impotent (Beckford 2004).

Mission in multiple urban worlds

Being self-consciously urban makes possible a greater awareness of the context of mission and the possibilities of wider engagement. Therefore 'being urban' for many will be about essentially who they are or the diversity within which they live. In the words of Robert Schreiter: '. . . people find themselves in multiple worlds of reference [. . .] Belonging is rarely as simple as having one point of location' (Schreiter 1996: 321). Within our theological and ecclesial practice in England there are new forms emerging. Churches are often growing because of new patterns of migration bringing in Christians who often do not have personal stories within a receiving denomination, but who will maintain a life in their own communities. The Church's mission alongside asylum-seekers has also changed inherited notions of identity, hospitality and location.

In the global North, urban mission has traditionally concentrated on industrial and post-industrial areas, where decline and depopulation have left community and church life weakened and impoverished. In England the geographical parish system has kept the Church of England committed to a ministry related to place and locality – it has kept us with people, when other civil society institutions and denominations have left. It has kept a Christian presence in areas which are now predominantly Muslim, Hindu or Sikh, demanding new forms of mission engagement. At the same time the Church has not always been flexible in its ability to embrace new migrants or those whose lifestyles are network rather than locality based. Understanding and engaging with the proliferating immigrant church scene is difficult. Dialogue and ecumenical engagement with such churches is not easy and markedly different from that which happened with the emergent Caribbean-led Church a generation ago.

Alongside this we find that the presence of linguistically different congregations within the same plant is not uncommon, with Spanish, Arabic, Filipino, Korean congregations developing new presences. New migrants from Eastern Europe are expanding Catholic and Orthodox churches, and infiltrating other denominations. The Church needs to understand its position on these faultlines of faith; the 'church of the poor' will not necessarily speak English or be seeking civic *shalom* in exile. This is a vulnerable presence often subject to physical attack or misunderstanding. Permanence is still a long way off for many; ethnicity and faith travel light – 'the collective of the future will have to master the art of self defence through mobility' (Millard 2004: 89).

The experience of migration is no longer relocating their sense of belonging. For many, migration involves a series of moves in search of work, education or personal security; aspirations always lie with the next move, while linkage exists with the many sites visited. This could challenge our understanding of doing theology in a particular place, as Argentine theologian Nancy Bedford suggests:

> The metaphor of place is both rich and suggestive, pointing as it does to geographical and social location and their fundamental importance for both the interpretation and production of theological discourse. However the metaphor has one fundamental limitation that becomes evident when we look at it from the perspective of migrants: its *static character* [...] What happens to us when, as a result of globalization and migration our *locus theologicus* becomes blurred in movement, unstable, not easily recognizable as a 'place' socially or physically? Where or how can we situate our selves to speak meaningfully of God? (Bedford 2006: 103–4)

Bedford's own response is to develop a theology on the move (*via theologicus*) that acknowledges not just the locations of faith but also the journeys and movements, and the ability of the migrant to speak from the 'there' as well the 'here'. For some, such as refugees and asylum-seekers, 'there' may be no longer accessible, and may be a location of mixed expectations and sorrows accessed via the internet or in exilic networks, others will be in multiple urban places across the globe during the year. There will be many urban people who find their placed identity to be multi-sited with churches of very different theologies and ethical outlooks. In this we find a diversity of contestations within which the Church's mission must find common ground in Christ (see Chapter 8).

Church and culture

Urban mission will involve immersion in cultures that are not dominant in the life of the Church. Those engaged in presence ministries or initiating new churches will find many questions of what is cultural rather than gospel in their expectations of lifestyle, relationships, approaches to the written text. It is not just a centralizing Church that needs to be aware of Edward Schillebeeckx's warning of the 'tendency to universalise precisely its non-universal, historically inherited, particular features tied up with a particular culture and time and apply them uniformly to the whole' (Schillebeeckx 1990: 167) of the Church. This has been noted in the recent work on urban church planting by Kilpin and Murray when they write about the need for cross-cultural empathy to understand and work alongside those with messy lives rather than importing received suburban morality and expectations of church life: 'Inner-city churches are sometimes accused of being liberal, but they have been dealing with such issues for longer than most suburban churches and have had to find creative inclusive approaches' (Kilpin and Murray 2007: 24). Writing from a housing estate context, Joe Hasler has noted that 'any urban theology needs to take the reality of "culture" into account if less powerful cultures are to break free of a suburban model' (Hasler 2006: 26).

Some network models of church pull towards the monocultural or interest group and if this is appropriate we need to be aware of how exclusion or the inability to connect with those who are significantly different might emerge. Hasler suggests that recent writings on church and networks fail to distinguish between the ways people in different socioeconomic groups network.

For many, the task of the kingdom will be building ecclesial communities which hold a unique diversity, often the only group or institution to hold that richness in the area. Diversity will not be solely about ethnicity, though this will be a defining factor for many urban congregations. In other places that diversity may be more apparent in terms of age, ability or sexuality, as well as economically or socially (see Goddard 2008). In recent years the emphasis has been on supporting individuals and families in their identity as minorities, but there is still work to do on the vocation of the culturally diverse congregation, not least at a time when there is growth in monocultural churches in culturally diverse settings. The diverse nature of city life may mean that congregations include a variety of traditions, approaches to faith and ethical practices that have not been nurtured in that congregation or location. The negotiated urban congregation demands a great deal of patient attention between members, though this cannot be allowed to turn the congregation in on itself.

Urban mission is multidirectional

An effective urban mission needs to take place, movement and communication seriously – it will be from everywhere to everywhere, it will also be within and among urban communities; it will be a mission to the city seeking to transform and evangelize unjust structures; it must also be a mission to other parts of the Church calling others to witness, understand and rejoice in the work.

Recent events such as *Soul in the City* or HOPE are not just about mission coming to the city but also how the encounter with the city and its Christians evangelizes others. A receiving community must have the acknowledged place as bearers of the gospel. Church Action on Poverty's Poverty Hearing programme allows those with little experience of poverty to hear from the poor and consider their own complicity. Those working with asylum-seekers have found the stranger to be the bearer of life and renewal for their congregation or community (see Snyder 2007).

The urban Church cannot survive solely as a receiver church, but must be aware of its own natural connections through the movements of its members; it also needs to bear witness to the daily transformations that it sees in its own life and the communities in which it is set.

Our effectiveness as disciples, churches as faith-based NGOs will not be judged on market share, Sunday numbers or access to telecommunications but on our encounter with Christ who comes to us in the hungry, the thirsty, the visitor, the sick, the prisoner, as well as the confused, the frail and the disturbed – our imaginative use of these proximate connections lies at the heart of our ecclesial life. The need is physical and spiritual. Many are alienated through the city's orientation to the market and a culture that dulls the imagination and bombards with images of celebrity and excess. Mission can be the act of creating space for an alternative world to break through, where reorientation (*metanoia*) can happen.

Performing and transforming urban missiologies

Recent urban theological writing has emphasized the performative nature of theology – we live it, we put it into action, we seek to understand our cities so our actions can lead to redemptive change. Theology must be a resource for transformation of lives, of communities, enabling the faithful to turn their discourses and traditions into discipleship. These must also be the assumptions of an urban missiology. We find the word of God in our lives when it is lived (performed) in our urban places.

These *missio dei* principles are enacted and embodied in the integration of our liturgical, evangelistic, sacramental and practical engagement with the kingdom and those around us. We also seek transformation – of lives, of cities, of processes – as we call people faithfully to live their lives under God discerned through scripture, tradition, stories, rules of life. For many, urban missiological practice will lie in the counsel of Jeremiah to 'seek the peace of the city' (29.7), an embrace, an acceptance of the city, with all its diversity and contradictions, as the context of a new performance based on redemption and grace seeking God's ordering is glimpsed on earth as it is in heaven. As Brueggemann suggests, this word for many will be a scandal – 'hated Babylon' could be the location, context and foundation of a new urban ethic (1977: 126). It cannot be suggested, however, that the exilic directive is about an alliance or partnership with city shapers but possibly more about the subversion of imperial city. The city can thrive only if there is commitment to its wholeness and well-being, where its welfare is recognized as being bound up with the lot of its exiles and poor. The theological practice we pursue in our cities at the beginning of the twenty-first century must surely reassert the centrality of that active pursuit of peace in all our strategies, tactics, acts of resistance, theologies and engagements as we seek to recover the potential and possibility of urban life in all its fullness for the city-dwellers of our time.

In this we seek the possibility of community where grace can flourish in new and dynamic incarnations. The urban Church can live only if there is commitment to the city and its well-being, where its welfare is recognized as being bound up with the interests of all its people and communities. As we have seen, that welfare is also bound up with global dynamics and responsibilities. These flows and relationships are often addressed in the work of Christians, alongside others, to reimagine their cities as 'fair trade cities', 'cities of sanctuary' or other imaginaries, as they identify what just living can mean for a place's internal and external relationships.

Everyday life in urban places will be where the concerns of mission meet those of 'progressive urbanism' (that's initiating good cities), where new possibilities are imagined and negotiated. 'Everyday faithfulness' will be found in what are considered traditional religious spaces but increasingly on borders and in protected and open spaces. New communities will be nurtured and God's new urban order will be glimpsed. Connolly and Steil write:

... to search for a Just City is to seek something rather more than individualized responses to specific injustices. It requires the creation of coherent frames for action and deliberation that bring the multiple and disparate efforts of those fighting against unjust urban conditions into relief and relate their struggles to each other as a part of a global orchestration . . . (Connolly and Steil 2009: 1)

The missional practice we pursue in our cities at the beginning of the twenty-first century must surely reassert the centrality of that active pursuit of peace and justice in all our strategies, tactics, acts of resistance, theologies and engagements as we seek to recover the potential and possibility of urban life in all its fullness for the city-dwellers of our time.

Chapter 4

New Platforms for Outreach: Developing a Wider View of Evangelism

PETER ROBINSON

The intent of this chapter is a constructive one. It is written with a passion for a full understanding of evangelism as part of the Church's mission but it also is written with a conviction that a space needs to be created for a much fuller understanding of and discussion about evangelism which will allow the inclusion of the experience of the urban Church. To put the case more sharply, many urban practitioners quickly discover that conventional evangelistic tools and methods are not applicable because they often presuppose so much that is quite different from the reality faced. What follows does not seek to undermine 'current orthodoxy' on evangelism or seek to replace it with another; rather the objective is to allow the tensions and questions raised by the urban experience to be explored in order that current theologies and practices can be developed and even deepened in their scope.

To put it another way, some ground clearance is required to allow a constructive and practical theological approach. This will be done by adducing ten issues that can point the way forward for such an approach. The intention is not to be negative, so each problem will be accompanied by a brief constructive proposal for further reflection.

1 The dominance of the global information society

A poster for a national evangelism course was posted on a billboard in the east end of Newcastle. It referred to the 'meaning of life' and to 'working 9 to 5'. It happened to be placed on the boundary between two local authority wards both of which had indices of multiple deprivation ranked in the lowest 1 per cent nationally. It was the time when the language of 'worklessness' was being introduced, where local councillors were beginning to talk about the fourth generation unemployed and when unemployment figures for under-25s were far too high. In the era of post-industrialism, available employment was to be found in the growing retail, cultural and service industries where hours were anything but regular and certainly not secure.

The dissonance between the message of the poster and the experience of social disadvantage where it was displayed drew sharp attention to a number of aspects of evangelism theory and practice. It was a reminder of the social origins of much of the thinking about evangelism and of the disjunction between life in London and the south east and the experience of many communities in the regions. The poster spoke about the way the global information economy, refracted through local regeneration programmes amidst the relics of post-industrialism, is shaping the experience of (un)employment into something almost unrecognizable compared to the industrial era. It expressed also the difficulty of translating one form of evangelism from a particular cultural setting into another.

One danger of advertising a form of evangelism is that the gospel can be perceived as one product among many others, and another is that its advertising potentially shares in the exclusions resulting from the global information society. As those who do not have material resources to participate in a consumerist society, so it is possible for individuals and communities to feel excluded by impersonal messages that appear not to be for them. At one level the advert was presenting the possibility of a course, at another it risked a potential dynamic of inclusion or exclusion dependent upon who saw and reflected upon the poster.

The poster was replaced in the ordinary course of events and no one commented, yet it spoke eloquently of the disjunction between two layers of city life: the layer that connects into the flows of the global information society and the layer that experiences disconnection and exclusion. Although in the east end of Newcastle the disconnection was mapped geographical onto the built environment, it is also a reminder that this duality is present even amidst so-called affluence, that connectedness and exclusion exist side by side in all situations in the contemporary city.[1]

In a positive sense, therefore, the appearance of the poster called to attention the need to find ways of working with the dual city and a stimulus to finding a broader and perhaps deeper discourse in the theology and practice of evangelism. More worryingly, it raised questions about the difficulty of translating practices of evangelism across cultural divides within Britain itself in a world dominated by the dynamics of globalization.

2 The changes in the city's built environment

As many of England's towns and cities have been reconfigured by social and economic regeneration programmes during the past couple of decades, insufficient attention has been given to the way in which the built environment shapes lifestyles and worldviews. The reshaping of cities and towns has brought with it not just an alteration in the appearance of the urban environment but a way of life that has been given insufficient attention in understanding evangelism.

In Newcastle–Gateshead, the dual city became apparent during the regeneration programmes of the quayside, beginning in the 1990s. Gradually, as the river frontage was developed as a place of cultural renewal and enhanced social encounter, so the inner-city estates that nestled behind the quayside were obscured by riverside apartment blocks giving physical expression to the duality. Such changes in the landscape and built environment are not neutral or benign forces on the city and its life. This has been argued by Timothy Gorringe who has written of the way that ideology has shaped the built environment, yet has also observed the ways in which new environment begins to shape these same ideas (Gorringe 2002). The contemporary city is both shaped by the values and philosophies of the postmodern city and also contributes towards the shaping of lifestyles, ethical judgements and ideas. As the postmodern city emerges, how does its development affect the Church's mission through evangelism?

One insight that is helpful in responding to this question is given by the theologian Graham Ward whose analysis of the years since *Faith in the City* was written offers a stimulating hermeneutic based on a discernment of human desire. Ward names the city of 'eternal aspiration', the city which was built to last, to create communities which were positive and to embody the perfect society. Ward also names the city of 'endless desire' which is the city built around a different end-view, that of investment opportunity, of acquisition of material goods and of desire that feeds itself (see Ward 2000: esp. 25ff.). Ward's categories find a resonance in the built environment of the dual city. The utopian dream of the city of eternal aspiration, and its failure, is found in the condition of many inner and outer housing estates. The city of endless desire is epitomized by the appearance of quayside apartments built for investment purposes rather than the creation of community.

The point is that to see evangelism in the city urban setting as simply the conversion of personal convictions of those with whom the Church comes into contact through its evangelism courses or church services or outreach events is deeply limited. As people's ideas are subtly shaped by their experience of what is around them in concrete form, so it becomes apparent that evangelism, the call of God to a new life around the values and ideas of God's kingdom, must reach further and deeper into the systems that create the contemporary city. There has to be a partnership between the accepted notions of evangelism and a wider recognition that lives, including our own, are shaped by the social, cultural and ethical views that are often not explicitly articulated but are embedded in the design and building process and written by the shape of the built environment.

Effective evangelism in the city must make these links so that the call to personal faith and discipleship is connected with and related to the wider conversion of lifestyles in the city and philosophies that bring the city itself into being. Observing the dual city at work is a sharp reminder that the Church has much to do in this realm and in its design of evangelistic methods.

3 The neglect of the precise setting of evangelism

Many urban churches are fully aware of their precarious existence, and one of the reasons for this is the constantly changing relationship with the local community. This might be due to an unstable population that is changing rapidly in its ethnic and religious composition. It might be due to the way in which the local church is perceived to be part of the establishment that has failed communities during the period of post-industrial decline. It might also be due to the relentless introduction of regeneration programmes which in an uncertain period of global financial change promote vulnerability for the whole community, including the Church.

Whatever the reason for change, there is a continual need to develop trust between the Church as an institution and the local community (Russell 2002). The constant development of trust is therefore part of the evangelistic task. Without trust, the task of evangelism becomes almost impossible, and inner-city churches are acutely aware that trust is required at both the personal and institutional level to reflect the way in which the high level of personal vulnerability is related to so many factors beyond the control of any one individual.

It would be misguided to see the intentional development of trust as pre-evangelism, since this implies a chronological process with evangelism following on when trust is (eventually) established. Gaining trust is not a one-off event but a process that takes place alongside and amidst the proclamation of the gospel.

Inner-city churches over many years have learnt the need to co-operate with and support local residents' groups and associations as they enable local people who are committed to staying in the urban areas, those who often have long-standing family roots there. Relationships with local residents develop through the Church supporting advocacy for the just allocation of resources in neighbourhood services such as policing, housing or environment. The ability of the Church to mediate and be an advocate in many places has been a key factor in enabling trust to be developed and conversations established in the service of God's kingdom.

In the east end of Newcastle the task of establishing trust extended beyond residents' groups to the wider structures of the voluntary and community sector. With the advent of a regeneration masterplan by the city council for the east end of the city in 2000 an embryonic community and voluntary sector organization met regularly to support community groups and focus a meaningful dialogue as small estates within the east end were designated for demolition and local people became fearful of the prospect of losing their homes and of the community's disruption. One of the goals of this embryonic grouping was to re-establish the trust that had been broken through a lack of consultation. The Church's support was one of the crucial elements and led eventually to the establishing of a formal community and voluntary sector structure that continues to resource the sector and establishes an environment where the different sectors, including the Church, might operate in an environment of trust.

4 The overlooking of the relationship between evangelism and church growth

Some evangelism theories assume that good evangelism leads to greater numbers attending church, but this is not necessarily the case because in the urban setting many other factors come into play and so this assumption matters.

The missiologist David Bosch has warned against evangelism being understood as church expansion and of a preoccupation with church growth that can turn evangelism into a mechanism for 'institutional self-aggrandisement' (Bosch 2008: 10–11). As Bosch points out, authentic evangelism may well turn people away from church because of the personal challenge and cost involved, but the urban Church faces compound challenges.

In areas such as the east end of Newcastle, urban populations have declined over many years as the density of housing has decreased and the domestic family unit has significantly declined in size. Housing stock built for the industrial era and now inherited by communities a century later exercises a controlling factor on populations, as the needs and aspirations of contemporary families are not met and population instability is increased as families move to other areas of the city to find suitable housing. It is equally true, and this is difficult for the inner-city priest to articulate, that some who find faith and begin to worship regularly then move away to 'nicer' areas. The realities of the employment market described in Section 1 above often militate against regular church attendance with irregular employment hours.

The reality can often be that inner-city churches witness effectively but are not able to enjoy the benefit that a growing congregation brings, as factors external to the life of the Church assert themselves. This is one reason why lifelong catechumenal models of evangelism and nurture understood as a 'workshop for witnesses' (Cartwright 2004: 481ff) hold such appeal for urban churches. The strategy for evangelism then becomes one of focusing on qualitative rather than quantitative goals with an integrated understanding of Christian initiation as new Christians are nurtured within the worshipping community. The size of many inner urban congregations allows this sort of integrated approach which might be characterized as the development of 'apprentice-disciples'. Michael Cartwright helpfully characterizes this model, suggesting that 'apprentice-disciples' are the ones 'who learn from other would-be saints what it means to excel in the way of the cross' (489–90). Such an apprenticeship involves 'mastering the disciplines of hospitality and gentleness in their relationships'. In baptism, regular Eucharist and the cycle of the Christian calendar, worshipping communities come to understand the patterns of devotion and ethical behaviour that are consistent with the pattern of the life, death and resurrection of Jesus Christ. The worshipping community in the midst of the diversity and vulnerability of human life represents an alternative means of engagement with the complexities of the contemporary city.

If this understanding of evangelism is to be sustained, however, a further shift in thinking is required, around the way God's activity in the world is framed.

5 An under-developed theology of the mission of God

The growth of *missio dei* theology in the twentieth century is to be welcomed, but there is a tendency for its development to be limited. If the logic of *missio dei* theology is followed through, then this means asking questions about the way in which the relationship between Church and society is framed. Is the Church somehow within society or placed upon or over it? If the logic of the mission of God is followed through, then what difference does this make to an understanding of evangelism?

These are crucial questions. To begin with, taking seriously the way in which the relationship between the Church and the world is framed will have a challenge to the language used. Accepting *missio dei* theology means that speaking of going out in the world or leaving the world to come into the Church becomes problematic.[2] It will mean finding a way of speaking that does justice to the fact that the Church is embodied in the world and arises from local communities at the same time as responding to the universal claims of the gospel proclaimed.

This crystallizes in the work of Alan Billings as he makes a contrast between the model of the parish church and that of the gathered Church (Billings 2004: 105–7, 120–4). The parish church model presupposes that the work of God is the welfare of all in contemporary society and the gathered Church presupposes God's requirement that human beings turn to God's invitation to repent and experience forgiveness. The point is that different emphases in the vision of God's engagement with the world and in particular human society yield a different vision of Church. Perhaps the distinction between 'parish' and 'gathered' models is overdrawn to make the concluding argument of the book, which is to advocate practical suggestions for the rediscovery of the parish church; but it is an essential contribution to the rediscovery of evangelism in the urban setting.

Another essential step is necessary, however, and that is to locate the Church and therefore evangelism in the overall purposes of God for a particular place. A *missio dei* framework makes a difference because evangelism involves pointing to the way in which God works in the world, revealing and making visible what God is already doing in human society, acknowledging that God is patiently at work in people's lives and then seeking to co-operate with God's pre-existing work. It might be said that this is evangelism 'from below' where the images are gentler and more nurturing than perhaps images inspired by proclamation and calling for repentance. Dan Hardy in his aptly named book, *Finding the Church*, writes of the importance of '*how* we find and live the work of God which constitutes, sustains and gives hope to the universality of the social fabric of the world' (Hardy 2001: 86) and gives expression to the style of evangelism that many urban parishes embrace. The local church in its work of co-operating with what God is already doing in people's lives begins to witness to the social order of which it is part, and hence it is a witness that may be recognized and is therefore effective.

There is much to do since at the heart of *Formation for Ministry in a Learning Church*, the report that lies behind much of the current reorganization of the Church of England's theological education, there is an explicit goal for the formation of the Church's authorized ministers to 'promote and serve God's mission in the world' (Hind 2003: 2).

6 The limitations of trying to frame the relationship between evangelism and social action

The way in which these two aspects of the Church's response to God's mission are often separated is symptomatic of a constant return to the suspicions of the social gospel debates of the 1960s and 1970s which often seemed to marginalize the work of the Church in engaging with social issues.

A helpful analysis of the distinction is set out by Ronald J. Sider (2008: 185ff) who identifies five typologies of relationship – from evangelism being seen as the primary mission of the Church, to salvation being understood as social justice and evangelism itself regarded as a political act. Along the spectrum of theological opinions evangelism is seen as one part of the Church's mission and as sharing an equal place with the pursuit of social justice. In the centre is the Anabaptist position of the Church itself embodying the changes it wishes to see in the world. Sider's reflections lead him to a position where evangelism and working towards social justice are equal in importance for the Church's mission: they are interrelated yet distinct, inseparable yet not identical. Sider's arguments are based on an analysis of the biblical word 'salvation'; he understands that social action may facilitate evangelism and vice versa, and that repentance includes the turning away from the causes of structural and social oppression.

Such arguments are helpful, yet at the end there is still a separation between evangelism and social action and a fear that evangelism is in danger of being eclipsed. Sider goes some way towards establishing a framework in which the tension is resolved, yet by his own admission the challenge remains that the clear distinction between personal and social transformation is based on a narrow understanding of salvation. When this is coupled with the observation that 'social action' is a limited category in itself, implying a focus on projects that support those who are disadvantaged rather than an engagement by the Church that seeks to address the causes of disadvantage, it leaves the question as to whether there is another starting point in trying to frame the relationship and a more helpful set of categories to understand these dimensions of the Church's mission.

7 The obscuring of evangelization

It might be argued that this starting point is the Roman Catholic concept of evangelization. It is clear that evangelization is a process, yet the framing of the concept varies according to context. An ongoing research project at the Margaret Beaufort Institute in Cambridge has identified four core aspects to evangelization – introducing others to a personal faith, reaching out to the wider world, enabling the gospel to penetrate all fields of human life and culture, and establishing the Church 'as the mystery of unity with God and of communion among people'. The valuable point is made that the precise aspect of evangelization emphasized will depend upon purpose of a particular act or programme of evangelization (Sweeney and Watkins nd).

One significant definition is that evangelization is 'liberation from everything that oppresses us' (Carey 2000: 221). The idea, though, includes the transformation of social structures, cultures, institutions, groups and whole societies so that they are aligned to the purposes of Christ. The liberation theologian Orlando Costas has helpfully related the transformation of 'situated' persons who are 'found, addressed and transformed by God' with the work of transformation in their wider environments, stating, 'Evangelization involves persons and communities working for the transformation of their respective life situations' (Costas 1989: 30). The outward movement of evangelization towards someone's life situation is dependent on the inward experience of forgiveness and freedom for serving.

One of the key questions that has arisen from the Church's involvement in a programme of social and economic regeneration from the 1990s has been the relationship between personal transformation and the transformations of the physical and community landscapes that social policy has envisaged. The concept of evangelization, while it does not offer easy answers, does have a distinctly different dynamic. Just as the desire to make the distinction between evangelism and social action clear grows out of a desire to ensure there is a space for evangelism in the Church's mission, so the idea of evangelization seeks to ensure that bringing people to personal faith in Christ is joined up to the transformation of the world. The claims of Christ are to be proclaimed to and received by the whole of creation, and human cultures and structures share in the fulfilment of God's purposes.

8 A new balance between the corporate and the individual

The sense of community is strong in many inner-city areas and yet many evangelism resources persist with an individualistic model that marginalizes many who continue to inhabit social structures where strong family and community ties still exist.

Not enough reflection has been given to working with groups in the task of evangelism, something observed by Vincent Donovan reflecting on his missionary work with the Masai in East Africa. He describes how he learnt to work with groups identifying their social dynamics and where the decisions were made. He noticed that local communities of Masai would accept and reject his approaches.

One discovery was pivotal: this was that the group dynamics which seemed to produce inertia in an individual could also serve as a force for good in the acceptance of the gospel. It led him to the observation, referring to the way that accepting Christ initiates a movement from despair to hope, that 'I know many individuals who would have never been able to take that tremendous step on their own. In community they have' (Donovan 1982: 88). Far from being a complicating factor, the location of the person within a community could be seen as a positive attribute. A recent evaluation of Donovan's missionary efforts has clarified that this did mean that everyone in a community accepted or rejected the Christian faith together. In acceptance or rejection, individuals or families were seen to act with or against the group. The response to the gospel at a personal level is still crucial, but the important point is that evangelism theory and practice needs to think communally as well as at the personal level (Bowen 2009: 79–82).

The assumption that the ties of community within the inner urban setting are either insignificant or fading away as domestic living units become smaller and individuals become more transient is open to challenge. The fact that it is often difficult to work with individuals in the urban setting is indicative of strong family and community bonds still existing. My own experience was that parents would often present all their children for baptism and sometimes ask for baptism themselves. This was true also at Confirmation when members of the same family would present themselves together rather than as individuals. As we set out to make working with children and their families a priority it should have been no surprise that the number of baptisms grew as families found in the church a place for celebrating not just the newly born but also family relationships. This is the reason why in the inner city the occasional offices offer unparalleled opportunities for sharing the good news of the gospel, as families and their communities gather for the transitions of life.

A question that Donovan asked young people on his return to the United States was, 'If anything happened to you, who would be affected by your actions?' For many in inner-city communities, the answer

continues to be a considerable number, and this constitutes an important challenge for the theory and practice of evangelism, a challenge that
will involve a greater appreciation of the concept of social capital.

9 The need to make evangelism visible within faithful capital

The setting of an individual within a framework of relationship is
central to the concept of social capital which acknowledges the relationship of the transformation of the individual to wider transformation of
the community. At the heart of the concept of social capital are relationships and especially the sort of relationships that enable individuals to
act together in the pursuit of common objectives.

Faithful Cities proposed a concept of 'faithful capital' to make visible
the everyday activities of the local church within a local community.
The well-spring of faithful capital is the relationship between God and
human beings. By introducing the concept of 'faithful capital' the intention is to make the Church's core activities visible as one aspect of social
capital, and hence worship, prayer, Bible study and commitments to
personal and corporate transformation are specifically named (*Faithful
Cities* 2006: 1.11ff & 3.39ff). This is consonant with the view, found in
central government social policy, of faith communities being reposit-
ories of social capital and especially for their buildings, people and the
relationships created through them (Dinham 2009: 5ff & 90ff).

At one level there is a question as to whether the notion of faithful
capital or even social capital allows for evangelism as an integral part of
the contribution a church community might make to a local community. There is perhaps not a major problem here. In a discussion on the
importance of local church rootedness, research is cited that highlights
the attention of church communities to the particular needs of people
and groups, of the 'response of patience and perseverance' (*Faithful
Cities*: 1.18) and also of the importance of hospitality (*Faithful Cities*:
3.42ff). It is not difficult to imagine the personal sharing of the good
news in such situations and that the telling of personal stories of faith is
evangelistic and in the creation of relationships actually contributes to
the social capital of a locality. There are therefore few grounds for thinking that a deeper understanding of the Church's role through faithful or
social capital categories inhibits a commitment to evangelism.

There is, however, a subtler point. Many church communities find themselves in areas of low social capital, perhaps the result of de-industrialization over decades or perhaps through regeneration of a housing estate or even a whole area of a city. As part of the local community, churches share in the decline of social capital at all levels – bonding, bridging and linking. One common pattern is that inner-city churches can hollow out with very few local residents attending and older members commuting in following a move from the locality. The bonding capital in this case can be high but the bridging capital (that between local groups, including the Church) will be low. This will impede the personal witness of individuals and even straightforward things such as the ability to invite local people in a meaningful way to church events.

If the local church community can develop an understanding of the Church's capacity to contribute to the growth of social capital, in other words to being a committed part of a wider network of groups, then it is possible to see how the analysis that social capital brings is an aid to building relationships that contribute to the Church's mission. The postindustrial inner-city networks that are created through friendships are likely to require supplementing through the creation of new networks through bridging and linking versions of social capital. It was this insight that led to the setting up of the Urban Ministry and Theology Project in the east end of Newcastle which networked four local Church of England parishes with each other, with the wider social and economic networks of the city, and with the wider Church. Essential to achieving this was identifying the need for the task of community engagement, initially a leadership role for one of the clergy, to work with both wider community and regeneration structures and the four congregations to discern and enable the connections to be made (Russell 2004).

10 Does partnership working inhibit the Church's outreach?

One of the implications of all that has been argued so far is that the local church has a responsibility towards the growth and flourishing of its local neighbourhood. For many churches over the past decades there has been a discovery of partnership working, whether that is a commitment to a city-wide or area partnership that enables the local community to engage with the decision-making processes that seek to renew both the physical environment and the stability of the local community. A commitment to partnership working by the local church recognizes that the church is called to take some of the responsibility for how the neighbourhood is, among many other stakeholders. In the active taking a share of the responsibility and playing an appropriate part for the well-being of the locality through partnership, there are many pitfalls and lessons to be learned. However, what does evangelism look like within the partnership setting, and does the partnership setting inhibit evangelism in any way?

To address this requires both a theoretical understanding and the confidence that only lived experience brings. The Manchester-based theologian, John Atherton, has contributed a great deal to the former with his understanding of partnership that highlights three areas of competence that are necessary for the Church, and indeed for other institutions whether in the voluntary, public or private sectors (Atherton 2000: 86–7). First, 'identity', which is that confident and well-formed understanding of our institution – knowing 'where we have come from, where we are and where we are going'. Then, identity needs to be embodied in 'resources', those things that make the partner visible and identifiable to others. But identity and resources are inadequate without 'outreach', a commitment to engage with other partners at an increasingly deep level through the sharing of key ideas and practices. Outreach for Atherton is characterized by sharing and dialogue which includes the incorporation of other worldviews into a relationship with Christian tradition. Atherton does not mention evangelism, but as with the category of social capital it is not difficult to see that his ethos of partnership provides the framework for the sort of human interactions that evangelism relies upon.

One example will suffice to show how this works out in practice. In the late summer and autumn of 2003 the PCC and congregation of St Martin's, Byker, identified that the way forward for their parish church was to work in partnership with local residents' groups, the voluntary and community sector of the east end of Newcastle, the local authority and other larger voluntary sector organisations.[3] The common area of interest was the need for an effective outreach to children, young people and their families. A partnership group was developed, with church council members working alongside local residents and leaders from the voluntary sector on a consultation process with the local community. A vision was generated for a way of working with a new set of relationships that would empower the community and church members to work together on an agenda for the flourishing of the whole of the local community. To support this vision, a new building was required, and within eighteen months St Martin's Centre was created that now supports the desired way of working. The worshipping community uses a flexible space for Sundays, and weekday services are held in a small chapel area that opens out into the whole building. St Martin's Centre is a forum which allows relationships to be developed on a daily basis. The church is a key partner in an organization that lies at the heart of the local community and seeks to enable residents to have a significant role in determining the sort of support services that are required and the sort of neighbourhood they wish to come into being. It is a place where the good news of Jesus Christ is shared daily and in a way that is sensitive to all who use the centre. Issues of identity have been addressed as the local church began to share the many resources it has to offer in a creative and contemporary way. The challenge remains to deepen the sense of outreach that Atherton talks about, but the platform to achieve this has been built.

Chapter 5

To Challenge, Relativize and Transcend: Proclamation in the City

PETER ROBINSON

In this chapter I want to investigate from the perspective of urban ministry proclamation through the practice of preaching. Proclamation is not to be reduced to preaching and neither is evangelism to be reduced to proclamation, yet investigating the proclamation of the gospel of Jesus Christ through the practice of preaching in the urban setting is something yet to receive enough attention.

Preaching in the urban setting requires attention because it is being challenged both from other parts of the city and also by authorized public ministers who are given the responsibility of preaching regularly within it. Some of the concerns about proclamation as preaching are described before it is argued that it is possible to be positive about the Church's proclamation through the regular practice of preaching throughout the city if certain characteristics of preaching are highlighted. The first characteristics of proclamation through preaching in the urban setting are resistance, contextualization, learning, discovery and solidarity. Acknowledging these characteristics not only makes a robust case for preaching in the city but also can allow new outward forms of proclamation to be imagined.

Challenges to urban preaching

The place of proclamation through preaching in the life of the local church is an important one. The Christian tradition as a whole, not simply the Protestant tradition, affirms the 'creative power of the word' (Avis 2005: 26ff) in the life of the church. A summary of Schleiermacher's thinking about proclamation – that 'an effective sermon is an epiphany: an appearance of Christ in the community of faith' (de Vries, cited in Dunn-Wilson 2005: 124) – heads in the right direction. Proclamation has a crucial part to play in the church's liturgy of word and sacrament, in which the presence of the risen Christ among his people and in his creation is revealed. Words articulated in the liturgical setting both communicate and act at the same time: if words not only pass on information but enact and achieve something as they do so, then how proclamation is shaped is an important question.

A view from outside the urban context identifies proclamation as an issue, and usually such a view is linked with a concern that social action takes precedence over 'preaching the gospel', so much so that the name of Jesus is obscured or even not named. Evangelism can be reduced to the pursuit of justice and there is often an assumption that proclamation and social action cannot be practically held together in tension as 'cousins' within the umbrella of evangelism (Abraham 1996).

A view from within the urban setting agrees with the concern that preaching or proclamation is problematic. This view, however, is more likely to be aware of the power dimensions of the act of preaching, especially in situations of social and economic regeneration. David Martin (2006: 103–18) discusses the role of power in preaching and laments the loss of social power that flowed through the pulpit (cf. 109–10).

The Church is still regarded by many inhabitants of the inner urban as a powerful institution and is often aligned with other institutions which have been or still are stakeholders in urban society. We continue to have many neighbourhoods where families and individuals within them have lived for many generations. Memories are long and the traditional institutions are often perceived to have failed post-industrial communities as worklessness has replaced unemployment and as the global market's forces continue to extract precious resources from vulnerable localities. It is easy to suggest that preaching must be about transformation, but how is this message heard when all the other institutions that impact on people's lives are demanding serious and uncomfortable personal and social change? This question is sharpened with the acknowledgement that churches themselves have deepened their presence and discovered renewal of congregations and buildings through engaging with regeneration programmes. The preacher's call to repent, to turn to Jesus and live in the fullness of eternal life can be easily understood as the religious version of the overall need to change. There is a real danger that the worst aspects of the secular understanding of regeneration can be played out from the pulpit, unwittingly but damagingly. 'You've taken our jobs, removed our dignity, and now you're asking us to become like you' is the cry from the congregation that expresses the deepest fear of the inner-city preacher.

The challenge is the development of an understanding of proclamation for the city that is adequate to meet the concerns of the two views. It must correct false impressions, if that is what they are, of the Church's practice in the urban setting by allowing the hitherto unseen to be glimpsed, but it must also enable proclamation to flourish throughout the city regardless of whether the setting is suburban, city centre, inner urban or outer estate. It must show how God's activity in constantly moving in love towards his creation, its signposting and enabling, are the criteria for good practice.

Resistance

First of all, for proclamation through preaching to be effective in the contemporary urban setting, it must have the characteristic of resistance. Preaching as resistance recognizes that the language of transformation is potentially open to misunderstanding in the urban setting and that communicating the authenticity of God's unique transformation that is offered through Christ requires a deep engagement with the struggles that inner-city communities in the throes of major social, economic and cultural change undergo.

Assistance may be gleaned from the feminist–womanist theological tradition that has recognized the need for resistance as a key facet of the preaching task. Writing about preaching as a ministry of resistance which builds on the foundations of weeping and confession, Christine M. Smith argues that:

> Though a transformed world is the ultimate hope that undergirds such a ministry if preachers listen carefully to the oppressed voices surrounding them, they will discern that the language of survival, struggle, and resistance is what permeates these messages of indictment and hope, not the language of transformation. Transformative language assumes a certain message of privilege and power that neither accurately describes nor reflects the lived realities of oppressed people. (Smith 1996: 45–6)

Smith's remarks on the language of transformation in preaching in situations of oppression articulate the experience of many urban practitioners and theologians over past years with the language of regeneration. Urban communities do speak of regeneration and even of transformation. They are acutely aware of the need for structures and institutions to change so that neighbourhoods may access a deeper justice. Yet, what is crucial and is at the surface of inner-city life is the knowledge that corporate and personal flourishing are linked, that calling for personal transformation without addressing wider social, political and cultural issues is a disempowering and even dehumanizing act.

Effective proclamation in the urban setting demonstrates a resistance to those things that inhibit personal growth. It even resists rushing to the personal and calling for a changed life because there is awareness that transformation has to be envisioned at every level. Proclamation calls attention to the struggle being endured and in doing so joins the struggle for liberation. The good news is that Jesus resisted the political and religious structures of his setting in the first century. As the new Moses, Jesus inaugurated the Christian movement conceived as a new exodus that is release from all that enslaves.

Proclamation creates spaces for human beings to be human and therefore to meet God in the midst of oppression, knowing that the promise of liberation is being claimed. It recognizes the ambiguities of the institutions that do offer support to disadvantaged communities and do this from a position of power, but allows space for worshipping communities to imagine a different mode of being that empowers practical discipleship.

Michael de Certeau's understanding of the city allows the preacher to see how this might be possible. de Certeau's city is structured by the 'strategies' of those who design and manage the urban environment. This is in contrast to the walkers who develop their own 'tactics' and do not allow themselves to be determined by the concepts that are imposed on them by institutions that attempt to control from above (de Certeau 1988: 91–110). If the act of preaching in the urban environment can be seen as a tactical act of resistance to all that prevents human flourishing, then that is a key part of allowing hope and even transformation to emerge.

Contextualization

Second, proclamation through the act of preaching requires the process of contextualization. What is meant by contextualization may be teased out through a distinction between 'setting' and 'context'. 'Setting' may be taken to refer to the specifics of the place – not simply the geographical features but also the particular configuration of social relationships that is found in specific place. Contextual theology may therefore refer to the neighbourhood, community or city which has a certain set of characteristics unique to that place.

In contrast, 'context' is a wider concept and is relational to theological reflection: to reflect theologically in a contextual way is to be self-aware in the way in which learning processes relate to 'the context'. Contextual theology – to take the etymology of the word 'context' – involves the interweaving of the many narratives that impinge on a particular setting. These narratives will be political, social, cultural, economic, ecological, gender, cultural and religious: they are structural influences and each contains a narrative or set of narratives, not all of which will impinge equally in each locality. Theology is done 'acontextually' when these relationships are not acknowledged to be present and do not inform the act of preaching. The cost of preaching without acknowledgement of the context (and indeed setting) underlies the concern of preaching as 'resistance' described earlier.

Effective, contextual proclamation must be carried out in relationship with the many narratives and levels of context. Johannes Banawiratma, out of his experience in Indonesia, has written about the need for Christians to live and communicate Jesus Christ in a communion of contextual communities, using the tools of the pastoral cycle:

> Contextual analysis and reflection exercise their functions within the community by reading the signs of the times: hearing, interpreting, and announcing the Logos (Word) and the Sophia (Wisdom) . . . Socio-theological reflection tries to offer deeper understanding of the actual situation (the hermeneutical dimension) and concrete direction or impetus for further actions (the ethical dimension). (Banawiratma 2005: 73–85)

Proclamation that takes contextualization seriously includes the act of listening to the multiple layers of contextuality, the discernment of which is influencing the local setting and a theological engagement. It is self-aware in its acknowledgement of the way in which the presuppositions of the preacher and congregation are shaped by contextual factors.

One of the tasks of proclamation is to enable the worshipping community to understand social, cultural and economic changes that are impacting locally. This means that the preacher will require the skills to both understand for him- or herself and to mediate that understanding. One instance might be the social and economic narrative of regeneration, referred to earlier, so much to the fore in urban settings over the past couple of decades. An uncritical and 'acontextual' engagement with the idea of regeneration simply taken from the Christian tradition leads to a serious dissonance in communicating the good news of the gospel to those whose houses are designated for demolition against their wishes or to community workers who are struggling to enable residents' groups' voices to be heard amidst the political clamour. A failure to contextualize in the act of proclamation is potentially disruptive of the announcement of the Logos and the Sophia.

Discipleship has a context and also a setting. The contextualization of proclamation through preaching is a critical engagement with the relationship of contextual factors in a particular setting, enabling those settings to be understood at the deeper level that is required for both the hermeneutical task and the ethical one within worshipping communities.

Learning

Third, proclamation through preaching needs to be understood more fully as learning, particularly learning about those who are often said to 'receive' the proclamation. It is at this point that the argument moves from context to setting. Just as the preacher in the urban seeks an understanding of the contextual narratives and their impingement on the very local, so an understanding of the setting in which the proclamation is made requires more analysis than is usually acknowledged.

A preacher is required to develop an analysis of the local setting of which the congregation is a key part. Leonora Tubbs Tisdale has written about the need for the preacher to be an amateur 'cultural anthropolo-gist' (Tisdale 1997, especially chapter 3). In the English setting, 'social anthropologist' is the more usual designation.

The task of the preacher is to 'exegete the congregation' by studying the cultural symbols of the congregation's life so that the congregational sub-identity is discovered. This is a succinct way of suggesting that for those involved in the ministry of preaching, the goal is to see God as the local community does and to understand how things actually are in its everyday life.

Proclamation as learning reverses the assumed order of things, but it would be quite wrong to imply that the act of preaching therefore becomes self-serving to those given the responsibility of preaching. Each act of preaching serves the whole Church. In worship as the church leads the praise of all creation, so the good news of the Christian gospel pro-claimed in words and the actions of the sacraments allows the world to see, understand and engage with more deeply the extent and nature of God's mission to his world. In local proclamation, there is a global reach from a local action.

Much of this reflection on preaching as learning is brought into focus by seeing proclamation as part of a local practical theology. The act of proclamation shares in the structure of the cycle of pastoral theology. Each act of preaching is an action in itself and receives a response. The preacher responds through reflection which informs subsequent acts of proclamation. Every act of proclamation is, in the work of Clemens Sedmak on the methods of local theology, an act of 'little theology'. Sermons are not preached to the whole of humanity, but as little theologies they are addressed to 'human people of flesh and blood with experiences of their own, with local knowledge of their own' (Sedmak 2003).

In the act of proclamation the whole Church learns. Proclamation understood as learning animates the Church as a 'learning community'. To return to the categories of Banawiratma, the community grows in its hermeneutical and ethical depth. Any notion that the sermon delivers a stimulus for disciples to put into practice for the remaining six days of the week before returning for further feeding the following week is sig-nificantly undermined. As the church community learns together about its context, the scriptures as they are systematically read in the assembly, the relevance of the Christian tradition and its own relationship between all three, so the community's worship begins to point more deeply to God's work in the world, and its efficacy as a sign instrument and fore-taste of the kingdom is enhanced.

Discovery

Fourth, if proclamation in the act of preaching is to be reunderstood as learning, then it is also to be an act of discovery – the discovery of an individual's place within the life of the Church and society.

The late Margaret Kane, the theologian of Church and society who did much to set the agenda of the contemporary Church in the north-east region, offers a definition of evangelism as the discovery of the place of each individual within society and the Church. This recognizes the Church's proclamation as reaching beyond the confines of the Church. It recognizes the reality that only a small number attend while many more still claim to belong. It does justice to an understanding of procla-mation that is a public act and therefore is free to point to God at work in his creation of Church and society. Margaret Kane wrote:

> To have faith in the God of Christ's revealing is to go beyond blind faith, to gain insight into the meaning of what is going on, to make a conscious decision about one's relationship to the world and to God's purposes in it and to find new resources in God. (Kane 1985: 46)

Margaret Kane gives a reminder of the link between evangelism and prophecy. There is an echo of Kane's thinking in the recent work of Alan Billings who argues that it is not everyone's vocation to attend church regularly, if at all (see Billings 2004).

Evangelism in the urban setting asks hard questions about the indi-vidual's part in God's salvific plan for the world and society. It does this because the contextual questions press hard in a situation where the setting is challenging merely to live in, let alone sustain the Church's presence. Proclamation, in whatever form, through a learning process offers the opportunity for personal discovery of one's vocation within God's creation.

This will only be possible, however, if the act of preaching, alongside other forms of proclamation, offers the good news of Christ as the dis-covery of the freedom which the gospel promises. Mark McIntosh offers a definition of spirituality along these lines which can represent the goal of preaching as discovery in the urban setting. He speaks of spirituality as a:

> ... discovery of the true 'self' precisely in encountering the divine and human other – who allows one neither to rest in a reassuring self-image nor to languish in the prison of a false social construction of oneself. (McIntosh 1998: 5–6)

Preaching that is authentic enables the discovery of the 'true self'. It resists the contextual structures and forces that prevent flourishing and creates a social space where the needs of people can be discerned and where the place of each person is brought to birth in both Church and society. To use the language of Paul Tillich, 'genuine' stumbling blocks to the reception of the good news of Jesus will remain, but authentic proclamation seeks to remove the 'wrong' ones (Tisdale 1997: 33–4).

Not all forms of proclamation that are evident in the city can be said to be authentic. One of the features of the contemporary city is the 'Wayside Pulpit' which attempts to make the proclamation behind church walls visible to pedestrians and those who pass by on public transport. Designed to communicate sharply the theological views of congregations and provoking either amusement or sadness at the sentiments expressed, they nevertheless testify not only to grassroots creativity but to the desire to make public what can too easily be seen as a private affair (Wainwright 2007). Intended to reach 'the unsaved', perhaps the 'wayside community pulpit' signifies the irrepressible nature of the Christian gospel. The unrefined theological sentiments expressed notwithstanding, the wayside pulpit shows how the Church's proclamation seeks to reach out into the high street, yet it is difficult to see how it meets the criterion of proclamation as part of the process of self-discovery.

Solidarity

Finally, proclamation through preaching in the urban setting is to be reconceived as both a means and expression of solidarity. The parish priest or reader who lives in and preaches regularly in the inner city knows that one of the outcomes of his or her ministry is the relationships forged through the learning process. It is difficult to see how proclamation understood as resistance, contextualization, learning and discovery can be complete without some reflections on solidarity.

The urban preacher will quickly become aware of issues to do with solidarity, becoming aware of his or her own solidarities and of new solidarities created through the Church's ministry. Dangers will also be discovered, particularly as solidarity can become a form of collaboration or mild co-operation either with social and economic structures that dehumanize or with an inward-looking church orientation.

The theology of solidarity has been illuminated through the Roman Catholic Church's social ethics. Solidarity is the key value which sustains human society so that it is worthy of human beings. 'It is one of the fundamental principles of the Christian view of social and political organization' and is central, through the application of love that serves the other, to the task of building the common good, enabling human beings to flourish and making society more human (Pontifical Council 2004: 293ff). This suggests that solidarity properly understood is a critical solidarity – critical in that love is the criterion to be brought to bear on society's structures, solidarity in the recognition of a common humanity.

Sedmak helps to understand that acts of proclamation, as 'little theologies' must 'challenge, relativize and transcend the local context', gently challenging and inviting hearers to go beyond the local (Sedmak 2003: 127f). Little theologies avoid simply reconstructing the local situation but point to new perspectives and even new solidarities quite different from the ones that inhibit human flourishing.

Preaching as part of the ministry of the word, in conjunction with the sacraments, plays its part in establishing the worshipping community, itself a form of solidarity. The doctrine of the 'communion of saints' points towards the solidarity there is between heaven and earth, 'the fellowship both of holy things and of holy people united in Christ by whom all things were made' (Ramsey 1956: 119).

However, solidarity may be also established with those who see the local church as a partner in overcoming injustice and witnessing to a fairer and more equitable society. This is because solidarity can be the setting for proclamation. In the east end of Newcastle one of the parishes decided to establish a base, in a disused shop front in one of the most challenging parts of the local estate – a square designed to be a hub of networks yet now suffering from a sense of abandonment. Worship began not just on Sundays but during the week. In retrospect there was much that would be done differently, but through daily worship and Sunday Eucharist and through the welcome of children in particular, the shop front became a place of proclamation. After a while a local community worker was reflecting with us about the church's ministry and happened to remark, 'You have made this place more human.' It made us realize that the movement of the church community into its new home had been read as an act of solidarity with one of the most marginalized places in the neighbourhood. It wasn't so much the words that were proclaimed but the proclamation itself within the act of solidarity.

Conclusion

If proclamation is reconceived differently, we can be more confident of giving a better account of the relationship between the act of proclamation, particularly through preaching and human transformation. If proclamation in the city is reimagined through the five lenses proposed, then perhaps the local urban church can be more deeply empowered to preach and proclaim the good news of Jesus Christ than it is at present.

Part 3

Being Saved in the City?

Chapter 6

Sin in the City:
Salvation and the City

MANDY FORD

The city is bad for you. Whichever way you read that sentence, it remains true. The financial structures located in downtown New York and London are responsible for the collapse of our economies with all the attendant financial, social and health repercussions that inevitably follow a recession, and our urban environment itself is unhealthy since pollution, overcrowding, traffic, stress and the lack of green space in which to exercise, damage people more than any other habitat.[1] The city is a poisoned place, its pavements and streets are toxic to their inhabitants. And it often seems as if the city is portrayed as morally poisoned in a similar way, as if its very fabric invites evil.

It might seem as if the city is in particular need of salvation, since cities have been portrayed as dangerous locations of temptation since biblical times. Babylon has become synonymous with 'sin', conjuring images in our minds of sexual depravity, material excess and the worship of idols. In the contemporary collective imagination, the major ills of the age – drug abuse, gun violence, knife crime, under-age sex and anti-social behaviour – take place in the urban wastelands. There is a frequently drawn connection between the urban, deprivation and sin. The Church itself frequently conflates the terms 'urban' and 'deprived' – and not without reason, since the most deprived geographical areas in Britain are all in urban settlements. While deprivation has become a technical word, it is worth remembering what people are deprived of: health, work, safety, appropriate housing, a sense of belonging, choices. Deprivation leads to fear, violence, depression, addiction, isolation, apathy, despair; or, to use other terms: anger, lust, sloth, greed, deceit, obesity and envy.

At least, the symptoms are not in dispute but perhaps there is dispute over the cause. In the 1990s when Tony Blair committed the Labour Party to being 'tough on crime and tough on the causes of crime'[2] he placed individual responsibility on one side of the clause and social ills on the other. The causes he had in mind were the social ills which influence criminal behaviour. Here was a mandate to tackle poverty, the breakdown in family values, poor education and other structural deficits in British life. Ten years earlier the authors of *Faith in the City* (1985) took a similar stand, calling on Church and nation to address issues of poverty, housing, education and social care in order to address the ills of the city. Although it is a rather simplistic way to summarize their assumptions, both clearly assumed that poverty leads to sin.

From poverty to inequality

Twenty years on, and the diagnosis is more nuanced. Richard Wilkinson's work on inequality has highlighted the significance of the gap between rich and poor as an indicator of poor health (Wilkinson 2005; Wilkinson and Pickett 2009). He has clearly shown that beyond a certain level of economic well-being the key factor in health and happiness is not poverty but inequality, and inequality is nowhere more visible than in our cities, where wealth is visible alongside extreme poverty. A trip on the docklands railway in London reveals views of marble-faced executive apartments whose picture windows look out on the Thames, cheek by jowl with brick tenement blocks adorned with crumbling drains and laundry hung on balconies to dry. These are merely the external signs of inequality, it does not take much imagination to consider the inequalities of health and well-being experienced by their residents. We live in a society where the gap between rich and poor is growing, and it is the structure of our society that contributes most to the ills of the poor. Though Wilkinson, who is not a Christian, would not interpret his work in these terms, from a Christian perspective this leads to the conclusion that we are all complicit in this structural 'sin'.

The high visibility of inequality in the city is one factor which contributes to the miseries of urban life. Another is the poor quality of relationships. Good relationships are one of the factors that can immunize us from the effects of the worst excesses of inequality.

One non-economic factor in health is 'a sense of belonging' which immunizes us against the worst excesses of inequality. Richard Layard has drawn our attention to the conditions promoting human happiness, which include social networks and relationships of trust (Layard 2005). No wonder that in cities where people live atomized lives, no longer surrounded by family or tribe, no longer rooted in locality, no longer on speaking terms with those on whom their daily lives depend, people are unhappy, frustrated and spiritually desiccated. Perhaps we should blame the city for the fragmentation of our society and the breakdown of spiritual values?

Whose city? Whose sin?

However, I want to challenge any diagnosis of sin which distinguishes the sins of the city from the sins of the 'non-urban', a diagnosis which focuses only on the negative aspects of the urban and leads in particular to the scapegoating of the urban poor. Like the disciples standing around the man born blind, we are busy asking Jesus, 'Who sinned, this man or his parents?' (John 9.2) and failing to recognize that we are all complicit in the fractures in the body of Christ. The condemnation takes many forms, ranging from the aggressive to the hand-wringing, but the characters are familiar: the hooded teenager, the single mother, the absent father, these are the scapegoats on which the news media focus. The Church has scapegoats of its own: the unchurched, the young, the apathetic, the resistant. Even more insidious is the scapegoating which implicitly criticizes churches with different theologies or priorities: liberal churches, struggling churches, churches which cannot pay their way, churches which do not attract young people, or whose members are predominantly vulnerable and needy.

Most of us recognize the gamut of reactions that result from being labelled a scapegoat. People and organizations quickly take on a passive, aggressive stance which is at the same time apathetic and withdrawn while maintaining a hostile resistance to all approaches of sympathy or help. There is little enthusiasm for engaging with the wider community, with democratic structures, or even with the local councillor, police officer or GP because 'they' got it wrong last time. There is little enthusiasm for talking to the big evangelical church down the road, because they will only make us feel small, or patronize us. In these circumstances, relationships of trust take years to build up and are rarely achieved in a transient world.

The most commonly offered solution to this situation of misery is flight. When people are given the educational or economic means of escape, they grab them with both hands and move out of the city to the suburbs. Salvation is presented in terms of suburban life and morality; security and stability, marriage and parenting, contributing to the nation's economy, lifelong learning. The division between the urban and the 'not urban' is perpetuated in the goals that are presented to individuals, and the cost to those who are left behind is not measured in the equation.

Regeneration?

The solution offered by successive governments, and one in which many churches have actively engaged, has been 'regeneration' – an attempt to build the kingdom through programmes aimed at both the causes and effects of deprivation. With hindsight, some of the shortcomings of regeneration projects have been recognized. Huge amounts of energy have been expended by professional clergy on regeneration projects and on all the infrastructure surrounding them: voluntary sector forums, local area agreements, local strategic partnerships, and boards of management. It would be unfair to suggest that these efforts are always semi-Pelagian attempts to save the city, but not unreasonable to suggest that they are sometimes motivated by a lack of faith in God's saving power.

Where there is a more nuanced engagement, Christians have recognized that God is at work in communities experiencing real transformation. In Braunstone, in Leicester, a community experiencing serious deprivation and at one time torn apart by factionalism fed by ancient tribalism, is beginning to see the benefits of millions of pounds of New Deal money in its area. This is felt not only in the provision of new facilities – a swimming pool, library, health centre and youth house – but also in the coming together of residents to clean up their open spaces, to reinvigorate a local carnival and to build relationships of trust. Significantly, the Anglican church has not only engaged with this programme at the structural level (engaging with the Braunstone Community Association in significant work of reconciliation) but also at pavement level through the work of a community worker deeply embedded both in the spiritual life of the church and the needs of the community. The focus of attention has moved, over the years, from the structural to the personal, and this seems emblematic of a change in understanding about the role of the church in the community among the wider urban Church.

The publication of *Faith in the City* twenty years ago, followed by a number of government initiatives in regeneration, and the establishment of the 'inclusion' agenda, among others, led initially to enthusiasm in the churches, which, fuelled by the Church Urban Fund, were able to engage in a range of projects which attempted to tackle deprivation. Many clergy became highly proficient at working in partnership with local authorities and grant-making bodies. After ten years or more of deep engagement with the regeneration agenda, there seems to be a greater wariness among urban clergy and a realization that delivering economic regeneration has not made an appreciable difference to the spiritual well-being of many city dwellers. A further cause of scepticism may be the government's annexing of 'faith communities' to deliver the community cohesion agenda, particularly as it becomes increasingly narrowed to focus on extremism following the events of 9/11 and 7/7. As public bodies, churches need 'a more nuanced and contextual understanding of how faith-based participation actually functions in specific circumstances' (*Faithful Cities* 2006: 13) and to look sharply at their own motivation.

Salvation and mission

Through all this time, the number of people attending church has generally declined, and urban clergy, some now ministering in areas with large communities of other faiths ministering in the predominantly indigenous post-Christian estates, ask themselves, 'What is the mission of God in this place and how is the church distinctive?'

At the height of the regeneration boom it was commonplace among urban clergy to talk of 'looking for the places where God is already at work' and joining in partnership. This has led to the performance of public theology engaging with public structures, with all the benefits and pitfalls already outlined. What seems to be missing from this discourse is the language of spirituality and conversion: the language of 'what God is doing for us'. It is as though we have forgotten that salvation is part of the divine economy in which the city is already being saved and its citizens have been saved too. Our task is not to save ourselves or our neighbours but to respond to God's saving grace already at work.

Without denigrating the work that has been done by faithful people in relieving the effects of deprivation in our urban communities in the last twenty years, it may be right to suggest that the Church needs to respond to changing circumstances by changing its focus. Just as the language of the state is moving from that of regeneration to that of well-being, the Church may move from the language of the kingdom to the language of salvation – though not by using that particularly technical term. The authors of *Faithful Cities* encourage us to see theology enacted and embodied in faithful communities. Conversations with my own, outer estate congregation reveal stories of release from isolation and desperation, acceptance after years of loneliness or alienation, renewed strength in the face of stressful responsibilities – all of which are under-stood as outward signs of God's saving grace. Salvation is experienced as reassurance, freedom, forgiveness and hope in the lives of individuals.

Colin Marchant, in a recent article on biblical themes for urban mission (Marchant 2004), writes about the centrality of 'shalom' as God's will for the city, encompassing as it does the ideas of salvation, justice and peace. God wills shalom for individuals, communities and nations. Significantly, shalom cannot be achieved by one at the expense of another, since it encompasses the need for justice and wholeness, for peace and unity.

If we start with the personal, with people who know Jesus as their Saviour and listen to them, we hear how Jesus holds them in his arms in a great protective bear-hug; how he walks with them through the streets of the estate; how he is present behind the security gates and in the darkest alleyway. For most people whose horizons are personal and local, the relationship with Jesus is personal and local too. Their relationship with Jesus overcomes the sense of alienation and isolation that is endemic in the city. The bonus is that once Jesus lives in us we are never alone, and he makes us strong enough to reach out to others as well. The tasks of visiting, healing, inviting, feeding and clothing are ones in which we can join in acts of neighbourliness towards our brothers and sisters, the refugees and asylum-seekers or the families struggling to live on low incomes. God's generosity to us enables us to be generous to others, as grace spills out and wells over from the springs that bubble up within us.

Frank Lake has written about the way in which grace flows from our sense of acceptance by God, to sustain us and then to enable us to rec-ognize our calling and achieve our vocation (Lake 1986). He contrasts this with the cycle of works, in which individuals and communities try to achieve status and acceptance by their achievements. Perhaps the cycle of works has driven much of the regeneration agenda, as well as various manifestations of the success/escape dream.

By contrast, those who know themselves to be loved by God are able to stand where they are, to inhabit their space and to offer their gifts without fear of rejection. James Alison talks about people inhabiting the 'toxic space' into which society places them and refusing either to fly or to flee. By doing so, they refuse to accept the role of the scapegoat, since the scapegoat must be driven out into the desert before the community feels the relief of release from its sins. Instead the whole community must work together to acknowledge its mutuality and to practise forgiveness.[3]

These responses to salvation seem attractive because they address the sins of the city as we understand them in the current climate. If the besetting sins of the city, and of twenty-first-century life in the developed world, arise out of our alienation from our neighbour, then we need saving, are saved and will be saved from alienation by faith in Jesus. If our initial reaction to being saved is a sense of our own self-worth and an understanding that we are accepted by God, we no longer need to define ourselves in contra-distinction from one another. We need a holistic view of our response to God's saving plan for the city. Our distrust of one another, between denominations and congregations, is simply another symptom of the structural sin which divides rather than unites the Church. We do not want a 'one size fits all' but to learn from the talents and gifts each has been given, not just to serve the place where it is, but the wider Church.

Models of salvation in the city

We have a predictable plurality of models of salvation implied in recent urban theology: salvation as escape, stay in your own culture and make the journey spiritual – which you might argue is the message of 'Mission Shaped Church' (2004), salvation as kingdom building where we work together for the redemption of the city as a holistic and partly centralized task (John Hull 2006 and John Atherton 2000), and salvation as relational, acknowledging local culture but interacting with it in sensitive partnerships (Joe Hasler 2006; *Faithful Cities* 2006). What is frequently missing from this discourse is a methodology for partnership between Christians themselves which sufficiently acknowledges the relationships of power which so often distort our attempts to work together. We are quick to judge and to diagnose and prescribe for one another. We behave rather like the friends of the paralysed man let down through the roof of the house before Jesus (Luke 5.18–26). The well-meaning activists are energetic in bringing the man for healing but the crowd is surprised when Jesus first forgives the man his sins. Surely he needs physical healing first? Why does not Jesus *do something*? The problem is that they can't see the difference that forgiveness makes, at least not instantly. It is hard to measure, hard to evidence, hard to count. The healing of the paralysed man seems at first sight to be a response to an individual situation, but its repercussions go far beyond the life of the individual. Like all the Markan healing stories, this one is powerfully symbolic. It points to the indissolubility of salvation and healing, showing us that sin and suffering are tied together, but not necessarily as cause and effect as we have sometimes understood them. The parameters of sin go far beyond the responsibility of the individual who suffers. This is clear in the healing of the paralytic, which reveals the power of Jesus to break up the hegemony of the scribes and priests and to restore freedom to the community. As Ched Myers has pointed out, the scribes complain because Jesus has remitted the debt owed to God, not because they want to protect God but because they want to protect their own authority to control indebtedness. The man's suffering exists within a structure of inequality which guarantees the benefits of power and wealth to some, while denigrating others. Jesus has come to break the structures of sin as well as to loose the chains which bind individuals (Myers 2008: 155).

The double-sided symbol

The sin of the city and the sin of the Church in the city are both structural and personal because structures consist of individuals in relationship. When individuals come to know Christ as their Saviour and to experience his forgiveness, their lives attain the symbolic status of the paralysed man. When churches live out their salvation life it also attains symbolic status. The question for all of us is how we read the symbol of salvation in the city when we are all involved in the structures, whether we benefit from them or suffer because of them. When Jesus forgave the paralysed man he did not stop there but went on to heal his body. It might be argued that he did this not primarily for the benefit of the man, but for the benefit of the onlookers, who in their sin needed proof that salvation had taken place.

As Jon Kuhrt has argued elsewhere in this book, faith and action are related in God's economy. I have tried to show how they are both responses to sin in our cities which is both personal and structural and in which we are all complicit, wherever we live.

Chapter 7

What Does Salvation Mean in the Urban Context?

JON KUHRT

Salvation in south London?

In 2007 the shootings in south London of three young men – Billy Cox in Clapham, Michael Dosunmu in Peckham and James Andre Smartt-Ford in Streatham – caused national headlines. Television and radio shows debated the issue and Tony Blair convened a forum with community representatives and the police to see what could be done. A lot of people were asking questions like 'What is wrong in our cities?' and 'What has happened to our urban youth?'

In response, Christian churches in south London along with the Peace Alliance organized a prayer walk from Peckham to Brixton on 22 February. The aim was to witness to the peace and hope of Jesus and to consciously declare this in the streets that have been associated with violence and murder. The walk intentionally walked through numerous gang boundaries to show that these boundaries meant nothing in reality because we are all one in Christ Jesus.

I participated in the prayer walk because one of the murders occurred very close to where I live in Streatham. It was both an uplifting experience and also a deeply challenging one for me. This was not an event which *tentatively* encouraged Christian values – Jesus' Lordship was declared boldly from the platform. And as we walked, we sang songs that were familiar to me from my church: songs like 'Our God is an Awesome God' and 'You came from Heaven to Earth'. But there was a huge difference in *how* they were sung. The context changed everything because we sang with urgency, passion and a sense of the immediacy of God that I have rarely experienced.

The walk was evidence of the church (largely Pentecostal) declaring salvation in Jesus in an unashamedly bold and vocal way. But this was a deeply integrated faith, committing to witnessing to God's saving power now; a salvation that is politically engaged and socially relevant. A salvation that is committed to both personal responsibility and the declaration of God's power to save our community. A salvation which makes good, and challenges injustice. It liberates captives from fear; to cast out the demons of violence and despair. This justice announces in word, deed and sign the reality of God's saving power: truly a light shining in the darkness.

Problems with our concepts of salvation

The centrality of salvation to the Christian faith makes it an essential concept to grapple with if we desire unity in the mission of the Church. But, as illustrated by the violence and deaths in south London recently, our urban context gives urgency to our discussion. We are confronted by issues that demand answers from those with faith. What will save the city from violence and destruction? What will stop injustice and suffering? Can we have hope in a better future?

Too often our use of the word 'salvation' and associated phrases like 'being saved' become religious jargon, flowing easily from the pages of liturgy or within internal church discussion. But those engaged in Christian ministry and mission in the urban context need to reflect carefully on what we mean when we talk about salvation. Are we declaring a whole gospel? Are we guilty, like many of the false prophets in Israel's history, of telling 'our people' only what they are comfortable hearing? (Micah 3.5, Amos 7.10–17, Jeremiah 6.13–15).

In his first book, Jim Wallis picks up this theme. He wrote: 'The churches have *secularised* the kingdom by identifying it with ideologies, programs, movements, institutions, and governments; they have *individualised* it by restricting it to the inner recesses of the heart; they have *spiritualised* it by removing it entirely to heaven; or they have *futurised* it by speaking of it only in connection with apocalyptic events at the end of time' (Wallis 1976: 93, my italics).

Wallis was writing in the mid-1970s in the context of an urban community seeking to live out the radical call of the gospel through counter-cultural lifestyle and political resistance. His experience of the challenges facing the urban poor left him dissatisfied with both the narrowness of evangelicalism and the spiritual dryness of liberalism.

The current divisions between 'evangelical' and 'liberal' mean that there is a danger of two separate and distinct gospel messages being proclaimed. One is a message primarily of personal salvation and the other a message focused on a social salvation. Our division along these lines tragically undermines the Church's witness because both sides are undernourished by the division. The truth is that neither narrow evangelicalism nor woolly liberalism are good news for the city.

We have to go deeper. The crisis of violence, poverty and meaninglessness in our urban areas desperately needs the good news of the kingdom of God. How can we share a holistic gospel which integrates the personal, social and political imperatives of salvation?

A personal and social salvation

Livability works alongside a wide range of churches in urban areas. In seeking to support them in their mission to their communities, we often discuss the way in which Christian faith has both deeply personal and social dimensions.

We have found the following diagram (page 76) to be helpful in discussing, and challenging, the dichotomy between the personal and the social implications of sin and the gospel.[1] We have found this model to be a useful tool in exploring what salvation means in the urban context because it highlights the intrinsically personal and the social nature of both sin and salvation.

Too often in history the gospel has been individualized to suit the rich and powerful and to deny the radical biblical critique of social and structural sin. This needs to be exposed but not in favour of a lop-sided focus that disregards the personal aspects of sin and salvation. This is equally ineffectual and dangerous. Too often middle-class analysis of urban issues (homelessness is a great example) falls into the trap of minimizing personal agency and personal responsibility in a way that simply does not ring true to real-life experience.

To avoid the pendulum swing within this false dichotomy, it is essential that we go deeper – to grasp the depth of sin's effect on the whole world and embrace the radical and holistic nature of our salvation in Christ. As Vinay Samuel has written, 'The whole of personal and social life is God's area of concern and action' (Samuel 2006).

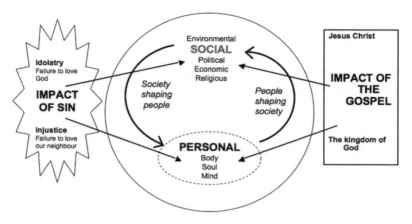

The fullness of salvation

The biblical picture of salvation is rich and multi-faceted. The whole biblical 'meta-narrative' is a salvation history, of how a loving Creator God is working out his redemptive purposes for the whole of creation. Within this big picture, we can draw out four interlinking ways of describing salvation.[2]

1. Salvation as wholeness

In the Bible we see that salvation centres on restoring the whole person (not just the 'soul') to a proper network of relationships. It embraces forgiveness in relation to both each other and God, as well as healing and a proper attitude to others and the whole of creation. A good example is when Jesus declared that 'salvation had come to this house' when rich urbanite Zacchaeus rejected his previous lifestyle and prioritized restoring relationships in his community (Luke 19). This wholeness is essentially social; biblically, salvation is never seen as a purely individualistic concern.

This is especially relevant in the urban context where relationships between groups are often contentious. The close proximity of different groups with different worldviews and perspectives frequently leads to fragmentation of community and deepening divisions between people groups based on ethnicity, age or geographical boundaries (as with the south London gangs). The salvation we have in Christ cuts across these divisions, for in Christ 'there is neither Jew nor Greek, slave nor free, male nor female, for you are all one in Christ Jesus' (Galatians 3.28). It is a wonderful thing when congregations make this truth incarnate across the amazing diversity of humanity.

On a more personal level, the demanding nature of the urban context causes anxiety, mental illness and exclusion of people with differences. In Jesus' ministry we see healing and wholeness go hand in hand, with the healings of individuals being the signs of the kingdom where people are fully restored into community (e.g. Luke 4.31–37, 8.26–39).

2. Salvation as liberation

Salvation entails liberation from oppression. This is most clearly illustrated in the Exodus story of Israel's liberation from the injustice and oppression of slavery. In the books of prophets such as Isaiah, Jeremiah, Amos and Micah (Isaiah 3.13–15, Jeremiah 22.13–17, Amos 5.11–15, Micah 2.1–2) we see a denouncement of the sin that is expressed and embodied in social structures that oppress and dehumanize. A similarly political expression of injustice is to be found in Revelation 13, where the economic and military power of Rome is portrayed as beasts which cause captivity and oppression.

Thus the biblical picture of salvation is both deeply political but also personal. In Philippi (Acts 16.16–40) we see God working through Paul and Silas to bring liberation to a slave girl being manipulated by her owners for financial gain. This transformative act leads to their flogging, imprisonment and a subsequent challenge to the authorities.

This challenge to the powers of the world is obviously relevant to the socially oppressive conditions in urban areas. The social, political and economic forces at work in the city which oppress those on the margins are not the true reality (they are 'false absolutes') and will be transformed one day in the New Heaven and New Earth (Isaiah 65.17–25, Revelation 21.1–5). Our task is to declare and embody this truth in anticipation of this age; to pray, act and struggle for liberation.

3. Salvation as forgiveness

A central biblical focus of salvation is on people experiencing forgiveness for their guilt in participation in wrong-doing. In line with the Passover, God has acted through Jesus to both conquer and justly forgive the sin of humanity rather than simply ignore it. The nature of our forgiveness in Christ can be emphasized in different ways (Christ as our representative, our participation in Christ or Christ as our substitute) but all involve the personal acceptance of guilt and the embracing of God's grace through forgiveness.

Jesus' death on the cross brings a deep reconciliation between humanity and God. Jesus challenges us to go the way of the cross, as Samuel states: 'The reconciliation brought about on the Cross has profound socio-political and cultural implications. How can humans deal with the bad consequences of human action, theirs, their ancestors and others who ruled them? Can such consequences be reversed?' (Samuel 2006).

It is obvious but important to state (especially in the current context of vicious divisions within the Church) that our experience of God's grace must overflow into our dealings with our neighbours. Jesus' story of the unmerciful servant illustrates this vividly (Matthew 18.21–35). Forgiveness is not about ignoring the wrongs we have committed but acknowledging their reality and facing up to our guilt before God and our neighbours.

The need for forgiveness and grace is profoundly important in urban life because we see the destruction caused by unresolved disputes and the downward spiral of revenge. Whenever I get my local bus I am personally struck how much the conversation of young people in my area focuses on retribution. I regularly cycle past the site of a knifing in Mitcham, south London, where flowers and cards have been laid for the young man who was murdered. When I read the various cards and rap lyrics left in his honour, the dominant thread is one of retribution and revenge for his death rather than appeals for peace or much sense of hope. I find reading them profoundly depressing.

Desmond Tutu's book *No Future without Forgiveness* illustrates the political dimensions of forgiveness in the astonishing and miraculous story of the Truth and Reconciliation Commission in South Africa. This is the saving nature of God's grace embodied in a political process which sought a truth and forgiveness beyond the reach of the normal process of law. It is a stunning example of God's saving grace which has had the power to save individuals' lives and whole communities from bitter and destructive recrimination.

4. Salvation as personal affirmation

The Christian story is deeply affirming for humanity, for we are made in the image of the Creator God, his identity imprinted on every person. It is this identity and worth that is affirmed through the saving action of Christ: 'For God so loved the world that he gave his one and only Son' (John 3.16). Of course, this image of God is marred by sin but it remains present in everyone. The life, death and resurrection of Christ does expose and judge the world of its sin but it also displays the astonishing extent of God's love for us.

We live in an age desperate for affirmation and acceptance. Anxiety is the spirit of the age and in many ways the default mode of the city. We see an epidemic of depression and the growth of disorders related to personal self-worth and appearance. The increasingly blatant marketing of plastic surgery plays on these anxieties in ways we could not have imagined even a decade ago. Again, we see the inseparability of personal and social issues: the demons of financial greed and corruption capitalize on the insecurity of the weak and vulnerable.

Seeing the transformation that has come over friends, family and the young people in my church youth group through conversion to Christ has been a deep joy. This thread of personal affirmation has been vital in the transformation process as people understand that the central event of history is deeply relevant to them *personally*. Reflecting on the threats and challenges he faced, Martin Luther King wrote that 'the agonizing moments through which I have passed during the last few years have also drawn me closer to God. More than ever, I am convinced of the reality of a personal God a living reality that has been validated in the experiences of everyday life. God has been profoundly real to me in recent years' (King 1963: 154).

The dynamism of transformation and hope

Salvation is dynamic because at its core it is about transformation and change. We believe that one day everything will be fully restored; that the world will be judged and all things will be 'put to rights' and that God will make 'everything new' (Revelation 21.5).

It is this eschatology that we seek to embody in the here and now, 'for in this hope we were saved' (Romans 8.24). Tom Wright puts it like this:

'*And earth and heaven shall be one*: that is the note that should sound like a clear, sweet bell through all Christian living – people called to live in the present in the light of that future' (Wright 2006: 186).

Hope and salvation work together. We have hope because we believe in God's salvation. But our salvation is worked out through having hope. I have found through my work with homeless people that the nurturing of hope is so important because of its transformative power. It is only when a person *believes* in a better future that they can work towards it. As Jim Wallis often says, 'Hope is believing in spite of the evidence then watching the evidence change' (in just about every speech he has made!).

In reflecting on his experiences in working to alleviate poverty, Michael Taylor has written of this dynamic between hope and transformation:

> By choosing to believe that the world has possibilities, possibilities arise where otherwise they would not have done. That is true of God and it is true of us. By regarding the world we know, marked by the chaos of insecurity, poverty and injustice, as promising and acting accordingly, it is filled with promise. Hope is creative. It is not the child of transformation. Transformation is the child of hope. It makes the hills green and it believes that all things can be made new. (Taylor 2002: 126)

Using the categories of salvation discussed above, we see this dynamic of transformation and hope through God's saving power:

From:	*To:*
Suffering and exclusion	Wholeness
Captivity	Liberation
Guilt	Forgiveness
Insecurity	Affirmation

Hope is a key ingredient in transformation. It provides a dynamic energy that is vital in combating the negativity and fear that can engulf individuals and communities in the urban context.

Conclusion: going deeper

Jim Wallis' critique of the secularizing, futurizing, individualizing and spiritualizing of the gospel message is a challenge to both evangelical and liberal doctrine and praxis. As he has said more recently, 'The message the world is waiting for is one of both personal renewal and social justice.' This is the good news of salvation that can be understood in the urban context.

Our creativity, energy and confidence in the message of salvation will be essential if we are to communicate it effectively. Too many of our church institutions are surviving off the fading oxygen of Christendom. We are in a different era now and we cannot expect people to simply turn up and participate in church unless they can see that the message connects and integrates with real life. Evangelism is now a political necessity if the Church is to be a transforming presence in urban areas. As Steve Latham has written, 'We need the real deal instead of the "decaffeinated religion" of postmodern liberal tolerance' (Latham 2007).

There is much to learn from how larger churches in our cities have been able to nurture faith, facilitate friendships, build community and run high quality youth and children's work. But also larger churches must not lose sight of their role in the body of Christ, and avoid the accumulation of resources and individualistic and concentric (Erskine 2003: 7) tendencies that gathered churches are prone to.

The crises facing our urban communities call us to go deeper in our faith and witness – to seek a unity in the gospel of the kingdom. And as carriers of this message and lifestyle, to become a Church committed to 'mission as transformation': places which speak confidently in the urban context of the wholeness, liberation, forgiveness and affirmation that we know and experience in Jesus.

We have much to learn from areas of the world where the Church *is* growing. As Samuel writes, 'The explosive growth of the Church in India has much to do with the discovery of the poor of India that in the Gospel it is not first the personal connection with the once distant God but the resource for transforming their present circumstances of oppression and poverty through a living experience of the Holy Spirit's power in their lives' (Samuel 2006).

Steve Latham believes that 'perhaps what we need is a liberation–charismatic fusion that will incarnate all aspects of God's new creation kingdom reality' (Latham 2007). This is the powerful synthesis that Martin Luther King developed and represented through the civil rights movement in the USA. And this is what I saw glimpses of in Peckham on that prayer march – a declaration of hope in God's salvation in the complexity of the urban context. It was exciting and challenging to participate in – a sure sign of God's kingdom at work in his world.

Part 4

Presences

Chapter 8

Christ in the City: The Density of Presence

ANDREW DAVEY

The church council of a congregation in a group of London estates talk about plans for the annual Good Friday march of witness. Most assume that it is something that 'has to be done'. But a dissenting voice is heard. 'Does this community need to know any more about crucifixion? It's a day-to-day reality. Shouldn't we be thinking about an event for Easter Day instead when we have the possibility of new life to celebrate?'

A preacher takes as his text the resurrection appearances in John's Gospel and the encounter with Thomas. 'Thomas was right – you only can recognize the body of Christ when faced with the hard facts – that is, the scars of the wounds that result from trying to realize the kingdom of God. What are the marks we need to look for when politicians claim they are working for a better society? What are the marks of solidarity? What are the marks that others will look for on us as the body of Christ in this place?'

The person and work of Christ has been essential in the vocations and writing of those engaged in urban mission and praxis. The radical perspectives found alongside communities of the poor, through faithful living and attentive reflection on the scriptures, have stimulated a hybrid, Christ-centred, urban missiology based around the themes of radical discipleship, incarnation and the kingdom of God. These themes are evident in the writings of catholics and evangelicals, as well as through the work of charismatics, liberals and radicals. Following and imitating Christ, seeking to be a sign of Christ's presence, bringing Christians into the city as well as altering the perspectives of those already there, are part of a common urban mission discourse – apparent in the songs of Iona, the work of the City Missions, and the Bible studies of community ministry agencies. Being among the poor, like Christ, brings dissatisfaction with pervading social and economic orders and a longing for transformation. Bob Linthicum writes of the transformation that becomes possible in lives and communities when Christians discover their calling to be 'a foretaste of [the] kingdom, a model of it in our life together, and work toward God's creation of that shalom community by being involved in:

• empowerment of our people as we together confront political systems of oppression and greed;
• equitable distribution of wealth so that there will be no poor among us;
• relationship with God and each other through Jesus Christ.' (Linthicum 2004: 190)

That relationship is forged through many encounters, interactions and experiences. Christ is encountered in the city in many ways: in the poor, the stranger, the hungry, the prisoner and the sick. Christ is found on the streets, in our churches, at the door of the advice centre, in the asylum drop-in or the women's refuge. The body of Christ is found gathered for worship, energetic in social provision, active in living and speaking alternative stories of faith and hope. Some will wish to imitate a Christ they find present in marginal communities, seeking to be an incarnational presence, living a vocation of deliberate discipleship through relocation, often discontented with the traditional church they find elsewhere. Others will wish to celebrate a Christ who overcomes despair and weakness, who challenges the powers and principalities that dominate lives and calls all to embrace a new way of living; elsewhere there is talk of taking whole cities 'for Christ'. For a number of years a group of diverse urban missioners, organizations, agencies and local Christians has gathered under the banner of 'Jesus in the City' to proclaim, explore and celebrate the life of Christ found in the urban areas of the United Kingdom. Some have felt uncomfortable with the title – it seems to be simultaneously inclusive, simplistic and partisan. Do we bring Jesus with us 'into the city' or encounter a Christ already there?

I want to consider in this chapter a number of aspects through which the life of Christ is meshed in the lives of our cities and the Christians we

find there. How does Jesus Christ remain the pivotal point in the understanding of and calling to mission in the city?

For some, the Christological dimension has been significantly absent
from the Church's major reports *Faith in the City* and *Faithful Cities*.
David Ford noted how the theological section of *Faith in the City*
reminded 'church and nation' (usually assumed to be those outside of
the 'inner city') that the 'teaching of Jesus makes demands on us' (FITC
3.1 / 470) suggesting an ethics and ecclesial life based on 'law rather than
gospel' (Ford 1989: 255) muting the vital dimension of Christian hope
found through participation 'in Christ'.

In a review on the *Fulcrum* website, Stephen Cox acknowledges the
difficulties faced by the faith-diverse commission which produced *Faithful Cities*:

> The report is about cities, and about the role of faiths in the city, but
> not particularly about Jesus in the city. This is inevitable given that the
> commission chose to look at faiths in the city (and I believe it was
> right to do so) but it has consequences. (Cox 2007)

For Cox, Christian participation in physical and social regeneration is
important yet it 'becomes very easy, if we are not vigilant, to substitute
something else, such as politics or community regeneration, for Jesus at
the heart of our faith'. The transforming encounter with Christ is essential for Christian action to be authentic to the gospel.

> Transformed individuals are compelled by the love of Christ into a
> fresh relationship with their neighbours, both their brothers and
> sisters in Christ, and even their enemies. This and the incarnation
> forces us, whether we are inherently individualistic or not, to choose
> to live together and to work this out in every sphere, including the
> political. (Cox 2007)

Christians will differ within the Church of England as to how and
when that transforming encounter happens (see Holtam 2007: 28). A
convincing encounter with Christ will be foundational for many urban
vocations whether it takes place in a conversion experience, through the
Eucharist, or in Bible study. It is often an encounter where narratives
collide, and through a crisis moment a new worldview and new rela-

tionships emerge. From the centre of Liverpool, Barbara Glasson describes such *metanoia* experience in a reflection on the healing of the man born blind:

> The story of Jesus is involved with the story of the seeing man that is about to change a whole way of looking at the world. When that reality breaks in we all begin to see each other for the first time. Connection leads to identity and identity to a new way of seeing. (Glasson 2006: 73)

But what does it mean to put the work, person and body of Christ at the core of the narrative of urban presence and mission? A number of theological concepts make this a pertinent question to the Church's urban mission: the mission of Jesus in relation to centres of power and marginal communities; the encounter with the kingdom-centred Jesus we find in the Gospels; the significance of the incarnation for discipleship and theology; the consequences of the crucifixion and resurrection; and the reality of living as the body of Christ in diversity.

The journey to the city

The Gospel accounts give much time to the journey of Jesus and his disciples to the city – their anticipation and excitement as well as the foreboding of what could and would happen. While time is spent in the villages and households of the poor along the way, the fate of Jesus is bound up in his clash with the opinion-forming city elites and their inability to grasp the challenge of the kingdom. It was for the city of Jerusalem with its contradictions of religious and political power that Jesus wept; in the machinations of that city his life was crushed and where resurrection life was glimpsed; and new possibilities were anticipated when he told his followers to wait in Jerusalem for the coming of a new empowerment that would take them and his life into cities that were the nodes of empire. That life we find embodied amidst the marginal, diverse hoards drawn and coerced into Ephesus, Corinth and Rome itself. The church's mission was not a movement against life of the cities but a presence anticipating the open urban future of God, when the old Rome would be overthrown with the coming of the new Jerusalem (Revelation 21). Living and finding the life of Christ in the city has been a vital challenge for the Church from its earliest days as urban Christians have lived resistively against the culture of empire meeting needs, offering hospitality, celebrating new possibilities of community, offering the gospel of Christ regardless of patronage or status, and holding a vision of a city renewed.

Calling and sending

In the Gospels an encounter with Jesus can send people in many direc- tions – some are called to follow, others to go home, some are called to testify, others to keep silent, some to embrace a radical break with pos- sessions, home and family, others to rebuild relationships. To go home is not to opt out of discipleship but to live as a restored sign of the kingdom break in. While those who are called to minister may experi- ence the need to follow Christ into another location, others will find that their discipleship lies in the familiar and the challenges of a faith lived in the midst of family and neighbours in their own Galilee or Nazareth (cf Kilpin and Murray 2007).

As Laurie Green writes elsewhere in this book, the encounter with Christ may lead out of one's 'comfort zone' to the places we resist the call to; it should not, however, cut one adrift in an ecclesial vacuum. Belong- ing to a church which may seem to represent and consist of the included excluders can be an alienating step for many who relate to the person of Jesus. The local church can all too often be an outsider which will be treated with suspicion if it does not struggle to be 'of and for area'. Bob Ekblad writes of the need 'to count the cost before naively trying to dis- mantle the barriers that people on the margins have placed there to protect themselves from hurt or abuse' (Ekblad 2005: xvi).

. . . on earth as it is in heaven

Jesus and the kingdom are inseparable. The conviction that what is hap- pening around him and through him is a sign of the new order, 'the transformation of personal and historical reality' (Codina 1993: 666). Moxnes describes the kingdom as 'imagined place', 'to indicate that it might not just be "imaginary" but also a vision of how a real place might be imagined differently' (Moxnes 2004: 109). Jesus imagines the kingdom in parables and deeds, and calls others to enter that imagined space and practise the kingdom through images and in places and tasks not usually associated with kingly rule – not least the villages and households of the poor.

Moxnes suggests that while the rapidly urbanizing spaces of Galilee seem absent from the gospel geography, those cities and the impact of their economic domination are implicit in many of the parables. When the parables enter the space of the urban elite, the space is rapidly reorganized (Luke 14.7–24).

> They are imagined places; they draw up localities with new social structures, freed from domination. They show how people are liberated to act in space in a new way, for instance, as honoured guests inside the house instead of being beggars at the outside. (Moxnes 2004: 156)

Many accounts of urban mission take the kingdom as foundational. Possibilities of a new community are explored in the here and now, for some as a foretaste, for others as an embodiment of the jubilee proclamation of good news for the poor (Luke 4). The inclusivity of churches, the welcome of the stranger, the support given each other, the refusal to give up, are seen as an experience of God's rule – 'on earth as it is heaven'. The disruptive nature of the urban mission narrative in the life of a church centred on its own targets and growth brings a significant kingdom movement to the fore. The mustard seed is a parable of such disruption – the mustard shrub is out of place, a deliberate and transforming disruption in the garden, yet becomes the sanctuary for a diverse avian presence (Matthew 13.31–32). A uniting factor among urban Christians is that they often feel 'out of place' within the culture of the church, within the neighbourhoods they are placed, yet they provide unique space for shelter and sanctuary. Difference is a key feature of the kingdom struggle; misunderstanding and hostility are the consequences of faithfulness. A disciple group drawn from marginal people will still feel that marginality acutely but seek to use its difference in a creative rather than destructive way as it practises the presence of Christ in its own space.

Incarnation

Incarnation places the concerns of the divine in human space and place. This demands a response and repositioning of our human concerns. Writing from the South Bronx, Alexie Torres-Fleming gives this thought-provoking response as she explains what led her to return to her poverty-stricken community of the South Bronx: 'God bound himself to the poorest of the poor, and in that he redeemed us. The theology of the incarnation mandates that you must place yourself in what you want to redeem. You cannot redeem what you will not assume' (Torres-Fleming 2009).

For many, such as veteran Methodist missioner John Vincent, incarnation is the result of an encounter and call to discipleship (see Vincent 1982). *Taking flesh* is the movement of flesh and blood into a particular space and culture – challenging and sanctifying, affirming the value of human life through demonstrating the love of God. It is as much about faithfulness in the mundanity of everyday life as the sweep of the kingdom amidst the powers. Through discipleship the kingdom is made known as the missioner identifies with the struggles and joys of the community calling others to join. Other movements in the city find the incarnation key to their self-understanding – the 'new monastic' movements and church planters discover the need to rethink how their mission and new social location need to merge if they are to embody what they are called to (see for example Haynes 2006).

An evocation of a divine option for the poor among marginal people often leads to an identification with the person and work of Jesus Christ 'who for our sake became poor'. Jesus was *Immanuel*, 'God alongside us' – maligned, misunderstood, marginalized, but holding in his life the very essence of life itself. For many, an encounter with that life is a daily reality into which others must be drawn.

This notion of incarnational vocation can be a call to cross boundaries and relocate socially, culturally or geographically. Following Christ must be a call to imitation – a *kenotic* vision of becoming vulnerable (Philippians 2), 'downsizing' as the disciples find themselves challenged about lifestyle, people's needs and socio-economic securities. Incarnation can mean entering into the pain and anger of a community, not always knowing where that immersion will lead, being 'disciplined by its disciplines'. At times it can mean being a counter-sign, standing out and standing up, offering a different set of values and beliefs which challenge those accepted by the prevailing order. Incarnated within a culture, one can begin to understand the power and forces which impact in that context and start a process of discernment for appropriate action transforming, reconciling, disrupting human society.

For David Ford, this roots the divine – embodied, distributed, vulnerable – in the human present: '. . . incarnating the glory of God is the face of Christ, the ultimate embodiment of a persuasive, vulnerable authority, freely distributed through his spirit' (Ford 1989: 253). Oliver Davies discerns a communal ethic embedded in the Church as 'the community of those who share the discovery that the structure of the world is changed through the incarnation' (Davies 2007: 55). This cannot be a cosy option where Christians can choose which social ministry they engage in. Being among the 'degraded or neglected' is a far from romantic option. The incarnation drives Christians to find '[t]here is no corner of human existence, however degraded or neglected, into which they may not venture. No person, however beleaguered or possessed, who they may not befriend and represent' (Stringfellow 1994: 164).

In Anglican social theology, incarnation is also about the possibility of transformation through an encounter with the divine within human society; if God became human, the experience and concerns of being human are those of the divine. In a quotation ascribed to a number of sources, a nineteenth-century slum priest connects the divine with the material – 'It is my belief in the incarnation that compels me to campaign about drains.'

Hispanic Pentecostal theologian Eldin Villafañe writes: 'Christianity can comprehend its God in Jesus Christ only through the world' (Villafañe 2006: 31). Through an incarnational understanding, the Christian faith encounters human culture in an open mode. Distinguishing between the dominant artistic, political, social culture of the Church and the gospel has often shut out the possibility of engaging and embracing the many cultures we find in our cities or poorer churches. 'God was in Christ reconciling the world to himself no longer holding people's misdeeds against them, and has entrusted us with the message of reconciliation' (2 Corinthians 5.19, REB). A group of American Franciscans describe their use of street music in evangelization as critical because 'if the Gospel lives in conversation with the culture and if the Church holds back from the culture, the gospel itself falls silent' (*Tablet* 2009: 18).

Incarnational principles are critical to urban mission bringing an under-standing of the human dimension at the heart of the *missio dei*, as well as the potential to discover the divine 'at home' and 'at work' within the urban culture and society.

Victim and scapegoat

As the divine enters human space and wrestles with its pain and disor-der, lives are transformed. As they find Christ alongside them, the victims of injustice discover the possibility of empowerment through the 'intelligence of the victim'. With Christ they are able to free themselves from the need to react through self-destruction, or a complacent accept-ance of their fate in a toxic environment. At the heart of this they find the gratuity of God, forgiveness and their role in the mission of God.

Catholic writer James Alison talks of the 'density of presence' experi-enced in the resurrection encounters as the disciples encountered the crucified and risen Jesus (Allison 1994: 23), and how that encounter enabled them to reread their story and that of Jesus from 'the victims' point of view' (39). Change is possible when a new narrative is offered, which breaks the old narratives of enslavement and powerlessness, and refuses to accept the toxicity of place (see Chapter 6).

Writing of urban communities and people in Britain in terms of scapegoat and victim is fraught with dangers of misunderstanding. The rhetoric of 'social exclusion' is still a recent memory for many. In 1997 the New Labour Government launched its Social Exclusion Unit with a leading theme being 'Worst Estates'. The title did little to identify the roots of that exclusion or distinguish between the people who lived on estates, the factors affecting their quality of life, or the built environment which seemed non-negotiable. Were proposals dealing with a virulent underclass, or the victims of processes and forces outside their control or the result of spatial configurations?[1]

Like many of the themes in the Unit's work, the question was never asked about who was doing the excluding or how those who might con-sider themselves 'socially included' should adapt their excluding lifestyles to enable others to be included. Who was responsible for exclusion – the excluded themselves? The undeserving poor are apparently always among us – the unregenerate that need regenerating. While the rhetoric used by the Government moved on to 'Neighbourhood Renewal', the attitudes assumed probably remain in much that has been written about marginal communities and the residual regeneration agenda (it is apparent that political marginalization has created a gulf of indifference in many communities; elsewhere years of paternalism or insensitivity have provided the ideal recruiting culture for parties of the extreme right).

Crucifixion is the moment and place where negativity and marginalization seem to triumph where state torture and human desperation meet. But it is the lies and toxicity that are nailed to the cross. Despair is taken by God and transformed in Easter as a moment of new life and hope offered to all: 'Though ordinarily the accusation nails the victim to the cross, here by contrast the accusation itself is nailed and publicly exhibited and exposed as a lie' (Girard 2000, quoted in Myers and Enns 2009: 92). Many in urban areas, however, still live in the uncertainty of Good Friday and Holy Saturday. Christians in areas marked for demolition and 'housing renewal' find they stand alongside others in the uncertainty of a community's future as familiar places and a sense of belonging are sacrificed and certainties are fractured. Taking the Stations of the Cross onto the streets allows that moment to be articulated and a new depth found. The story must be told. False resurrections are promised, planning blight and recession strangle communities. It is in such places that we need to discover a proclamation that carries the conviction that with or through the work of Christ crucified, God's love (grace) continues to flow to all people who need a new life of love and respect, for which Christ lived and died. Easter is possible.

The body

When we talk about the Church we designate the local congregation and the Church universal as the body of Christ reimagined for our time and place. Our encounter with Christ incorporates us *en Christou* (in Christ) with others regardless of culture and status to live altruistically with respect for others in diversity. 'In Christ there is neither Jew nor Greek . . .', the body is a place where pain can be shared and the suspicion of difference overcome. James Allison writes, 'Believers are supposed to live like Christ, proclaiming Christ's death in which they participate and sharing his radical vision of God's love for all people' (Allison 1994: 101).

Christian educationalists often use scriptural and cultural images of Jesus to encourage a deeper understanding of the person of Christ within a globally diverse Church).[2] Recent elections saw the British National Party using the image of Christ as an ethnic totem, criticizing a Church it claimed had sold out to liberal immigration policies and multiculturalism. A campaign opposing the BNP illustrated the possible impact of BNP repatriation policies with a team photo of the England football team, with those who would not meet the BNP's criteria blanked. A priest in Manchester told me of a conversation with a congregation member who considered voting BNP, despite emphatically stating his commitment to a multi-ethnic congregation – he was challenged by the question, 'Who would be missing from our congregation if BNP policies were introduced?' I know other clergy were asking similar questions. Who would be missing from the body of Christ in this place? What would become of our cosmopolitan churches? Where would be the asylum-seekers and those with irregular status supported and advocated by their congregations? And what of those who were newcomers in urban and rural areas which had no previous experience of migration? The Aryan Christ of the BNP poster is not the human face found in very real manifestations of the body of Christ across the cities of Britain, where diversity is celebrated and not a cause for enmity. The Aryan Christ of the BNP can only offer division and indifference to the new neighbour and the needy.

As many urban congregations know, being the body of Christ is a cause for the celebration of a diversity that enables the fear of the strange to be overcome. The dynamics of congregational life need negotiation if they are to be a sign of real solidarity. To live as a body means to live in diversity, not an imposed single culture or function, but through solidarity, resisting self-seeking individualism. Being Christ to each other and to those beyond creates the challenge to be constantly negotiating and transforming ourselves towards a new humanity. 'Being in Christ is a creative struggling space not a boundary marker' (Kim 2009: 102); handling power reimagined must never mean imitating the way power has been used in the past and revisiting memories with retribution in mind.

> . . . the memory is not a struggle to gain the upper hand for a set of ethnic and cultural traditions, previously enslaved; rather it was to cause a diversity of culture and oppression and made, instead, into a shared experience and resource for the inclusion of all people into a common future. (Selby 1995: 60)

Yung Suk Kim sees the potential of the body metaphor in similar terms to Moxnes' perception of the kingdom. Using terms familiar to urban theorists, Kim describes the modal nature of the body of Christ as '"third space" of a community that is struggling toward liberation and justice for all . . . realized when humans live in that struggling space and time' (Kim 2009: 38).

To be Christ for an area is the fundamental mission of the urban church. In most aspects a flesh and blood group is visibly little different from others but the body of Christ performs its vision of the kingdom in the midst of its pain of divisions through a realistic and radical participation with the lowly in Christ's suffering (Kim 2009: 37/38). The much-used prayer of St Theresa of Avila reminds us that Christ has no body on earth but ours.

The negotiating praxis of the body of Christ must be based on all for one another (Romans 12.16; 1 Thessalonians 5.15) – the discovery of community offers a Christ-based alternative within the tensions of living across difference, the possibility of a redeemed, regenerated humanity. The body is found in the metaphor of household and living temple. Christ remains as cornerstone – the stability when what are thought to be the load-bearing walls of enmity come crashing down (Ephesians 2). Reflecting on the letter to the Ephesians, Myers and Enns write of how the 'structural integrity' of an undivided house is compromised by the 'social architecture of our cities'. Church members:

> . . . cannot by definition, co-operate with any of the myriad social constructions of enmity. [. . .] Despite the fact that walls still exist in the world, Christians should live as if they have been torn down. If we are not involved in defying walls of division – even if they are load-bearing walls – the church is not being the church, no matter what it calls itself. (Myers and Enns 2009: 93)

For many urban churches this has implications as congregational identities shift and congregations are renewed. It also demands openness to those who come without any previous experience of faith or community, those whose difference or newness might otherwise be feared. It offers a glimpse of ourselves embodying God's open future in a partitioned city, maybe in places where that future is rarely spoken of. With Christ as cornerstone we can be part of the fabric of a transformed city offering the possibility (to use urbanist Peter Marcuse's words) 'of full, free unfragmented lives, not cities of discretion and domination; we need walls that welcome and shelter, not walls that exclude and oppress' (Marcuse 1995: 251).

To be Christ and to follow Christ in the cities of the twenty-first century is our Christian calling. To explicitly acknowledge the call of Christ brings disciples and enemies close to the mystery of the incarnation and cross. It is from the cross that imagining and building a new city becomes possible; the body of Christ will bear the marks of vilification if it believes human transformation to be truly possible. To acknowledge Christ as our urban contemporary remains fundamental within our urban missiology as the kingdom is lived, spoken and embodied in our contemporary cities.

Chapter 9

God is a Group?: The Persistent Presence of the Holy Spirit

LAURIE GREEN

There's no doubt that if you want to meet Jesus, you will find him in the urban poor. That has been my abiding experience throughout 40 years of urban ministry and urban theological endeavour. Jesus is around every corner, celebrating in the skill and daring of the kid on the skateboard, devastated in the despair of the local prostitute, encouraged in the neighbourhood tenants' meeting, bustling with the volunteers in the soup kitchen, crying with the abused child of the addict, sitting quietly with the few who gather for Morning Service in the cold street-corner church, dancing with the swaying choirs of the pentecostal singers. You will find him in the faces of individuals who are experiencing life at the edge, you will know him present in the groups who seek to bring peace on the streets or fair play in the town council. You don't so much have to look for Jesus in the city or the housing estate, he comes and finds you!

Jesus told us to expect these personal encounters with him among the downtrodden (for example in Matthew 25.37–40) but it's not only when you're with the urban poor that you can sense his presence. You can be touched by his saddened amazement at the profligacy of the city bankers and his pity for the self-importance of the banqueting city dignitaries. For when the angel names Jesus 'Emmanuel' (Matthew 1.23), meaning 'God with us', being with us means that he sees right through us, rich and poor alike!

In an earlier chapter Andrew Davey comments that so much of the more recent writing of urban theologians is about the presence of 'Jesus in the city' – he is simply so evident. But in this chapter I am concerned to go behind the person of Jesus and ask how we might understand what his Holy Spirit is doing among the urban people of Britain.

The Holy Spirit of God is in the world, seeking, among other things, to bring about the restoration in us of the image of God in which we were originally made. In so many ways we have marred that image through injustice, greed or self-aggrandizement. But it is still there in us, and the Holy Spirit seeks to bring that to light through the gifts of grace and power. So the Spirit of God is a disturbing Spirit who will not leave us alone or at rest. And not only does the Spirit yearn for the restoration of human beings but of the whole created order – matter and structure – for the world itself is fallen and it too is in process of regeneration by the gifts of grace. So we can walk around the city of Jerusalem, and while one part of us may spy out the horrors of how it falls pathetically short of all that we may hope for in that Holy City, the other half of us may see repeated glimpses of the dramatic beauty and serenity of the place. The Spirit works to bring the New Jerusalem into our midst just as the Spirit is active to bring about our more personal regeneration.

The God in whose image we are created is the vibrant Holy Trinity – a dynamic interpersonal relationship of Father, Son and Holy Spirit – and so it is not in the Spirit's essential nature to work for this regeneration and restoration independently of us. God always draws us in and yearns for our responsive partnership, knowing that we are created in God's image as collaborators, as social beings, and that if we are to find again that Godly nature within us, then we will wish to work with God and one another for the restoration of our cities and our societal life together.

But the dynamic of human relationships is far from the all-loving and mutually deferential *perichoresis* which is inherent in the Trinitarian Godhead! Fallen we are indeed, and yet glimpses of who we should be still shine through. Likewise, that most complex expression of human relationship, the city, is full of highs and lows, and that is itself an expressive picture of what it is to be human. Walk round a city and explore its many facets and teeming life. It's full of vibrant money-making and music-making, and it's full of oppressive selfishness and dirt. Glory at its colour and mixity, deplore its tragedy and waste of lives. Rejoice at its chaotic order and wonder at its detailed vastness. What has humankind created here in its cities – and what does God see? When Jesus weeps for the city he opens to us his longing, his frustrated despair and his hope for what we are and what we might become. So he offers us his Holy Spirit to guide, challenge and charge us to remake our complex urban society in the image of the Triune God. And it is the relational Holy Trinity of God who relies on us to respond.

I want to explore how some of this actually happens at pavement level, and in doing so I make a number of assumptions, not least that God is continually trying to break through to us and that God, despite the divine transcendent nature, is prepared to accommodate to our condition and context, the Spirit condescending to be Emmanuel – God with us.

A super-abundance of grace

Where on earth does the resilience of ordinary people come from when we see them confronted with the most awful circumstances? Go into Stratford Market in east London and see the single mum pushing the buggy with two other toddlers tagging along behind as she tries desperately to search out some cheap shoes and a toy. Listen to the loud anguished mobile phone conversation as the young black guy pleads in every way he knows how, to secure some casual labour for the week. See the recently arrived asylum-seeker family looking totally lost as they make their way from stall to stall in the hope of some help in such a foreign culture. Try to ignore the trembling hands of the beggars and their wide-eyed stare as the anxiety for their next hit absorbs them. Exploited or ignored people struggle to survive in harsh urban settings and find themselves at the mercy of multiplying deprivation. Only those who are near to such people recognize just what 'multiple' deprivation can really mean as one thing just piles upon the next in an unmitigated deluge of 'bad luck' and disaster.

Go back in a week or two and the same people are there. They've managed to make it through the days – to overcome the terrifying challenges of each day. These are indeed people of faith and resilience – they have faith in the fact that challenges of this magnitude are sufferable. And sometimes, just sometimes, we'll see the same people but now looking more whole and together as human beings. Something or 'someone' has happened for them and they have been given the strength and energy to rise again. If you live with the poor, then you become the observer of constant miracles. We sense the Holy Spirit at work in these people's lives, certainly in those who have experienced relief from their burden, but also in those who have, against all the odds, found the courage to endure. Sometimes, too, we also have the honour to see Spirit-inspired acts of regeneration and unexpected grace through ordinary people's resistance – the woman who patiently teaches local children to cook or draw, a man taking time to talk to the hoodies on the bus, or the team of street pastors in the midst of the night-time economy of the city centre. There are plenty of Spirit-filled angels on the streets.

Spirit-filled places

There are plenty of what we might call 'thin places' too. A 'thin place' is where the gap between the obvious and the mystery is wafer-thin; where the Holy Spirit of God is very close even though you may find yourself for all the world in a very ordinary place. Suddenly you become aware of the fascinating beauty of the squalid factory, or the juxtaposition of the grey tower-block and the radiant red sky surrounding it, the reflective puddle in the empty market – thin places promising that salvation of the physical environment is indeed possible.

Justice or patience?

Of course, I am not poor nor materially oppressed, and so I must guard against romanticizing the plight of the downtrodden or the deplorable physical environment in which people are expected to live. But it seems that the Holy Spirit of God in Christ can and often does direct me from my safe and more objective situation to look 'dispassionately' for the causes of the atrocious conditions of the poor. So while I cannot directly identify with the urban oppressed, the Spirit graciously gives me a particular way of playing my part in identifying and changing the causes of their condition. And this part is offered to me by virtue of my objective distance as 'not really poor', even if I live and work in the midst of oppressed people. But with this privilege, there is laid upon me by the Spirit the responsibility not merely to use my knowledge of poverty as a means to look informed and cool but to inspire in me an aching desire for justice – such is the imperative of the Spirit's compassionate touch upon the soul.

For the urban poor, the situation is entirely different. For while I am able to make decisions and take actions from my privileged place, their experience is largely one of waiting upon change in others before they can be at liberty to experience what they want to become. My mother is 93 and a visit with her to her GP surgery in east London is an education. On the wall is posted a notice which says that locals should not, if possible, bother the doctor with back pain and a whole list of other ailments, because the doctors simply don't have time to be consulted. Visit the job centre in Southend and feel the same desperate waiting for others to choose what your life will be. Sitting there and waiting brings to mind the Psalmist's cry, 'How long O Lord, will you forget me? . . . How long must I nurse rebellion in my soul, sorrow in my heart day and night? How long is the enemy to domineer over me? . . . As for me, I trust in your faithful love, O Lord' (Psalm 13). The poor must learn patience at injustice or learn the arts of rebellion, lest they fall into despondency of spirit. This is stark and thoroughly unjust, but true – and if this containment is truly the lot of the poor, we are forced to the question of whether or not rebellion is an intention of the Holy Spirit.

The spirit of connectivity

It is important for us to recognize here that, however much we pretend as a society that the poor are separate from the mainstream of society (they certainly are well hidden in Britain), they are in fact related directly to the rich. It is again the Holy Spirit's connectedness as a person within the Holy Trinity that signals to us that we are made in that same image of interdependence – 'of one being' with one another. If someone despairs because they are alone, it is because of desertion, not because it is intended that there is no one for them. This is why in the famous story from the Hebrew scriptures (Genesis 18.1–16) of the visit of the three angels, the Christian interpretation of the event often assumes that the three were indeed the three persons of the Holy Trinity. This is why, although the three figures were visitors, they were mysteriously also hosts. Rublev, the famous Russian icon painter, depicted the three seated around the table where the bodily posture of the Holy Spirit beckons the viewer into the gathering. The Holy Spirit is the visitor who welcomes us in. It is this radical hospitality of the Spirit which invites us into God – just as the Blessed Virgin Mary is visited by the angel who tells of the overwhelming visitation of the Spirit who will welcome her into God's purposes.

The Spirit is the source of this hospitality and we can sometimes

glimpse something of it in the way in which aliens are not merely toler-
ated but cherished at the margins of urban society. Now and again,
amidst all the hatred, there is the most amazing kindness and intercourse
between those who understand themselves as the host community and
those newly arrived. What always impresses me about New York is that
it is a city where so many see themselves as hosts and, at the same time,
guests. But such cherishing of the alien demands conversion of the heart
to the common good – and this, as we have seen, is a grace given by the
third person of the Holy Trinity – the Spirit. This radical hospitality is
also explored among urban Christians as they tentatively approach one
another. When we compare the extraordinary variety and diversity of
groups newly arriving in our inner cities, it is sometimes difficult to see
what they could possibly hold in common, and yet there are signs of a
tremendous risk being taken by Christians in recent months and years,
in seeking to learn from the otherness – even worshipping and praying
together across deep divides of ethnicity and culture. There seems little
to connect such diverse Christian groups, apart from the grace of the
Holy Spirit.

The Holy Spirit and power

While the power of the Spirit is to be experienced in this abundant grace,
we can also recognize in the urban situation the presence of God's Spirit
in the powerlessness of many. Any observer must admit that so often the
power of death conquers in the city – poverty, bad housing, the com-
modification of the young and so on. We wonder just how God relates
to the despair, the disorder and meaninglessness. How does God view
the abandoned shops, the workers in the cheap-labour sweat shops, the
TV culture dulling the imaginative creativity, the designer label celebrity
and the excess, or the regeneration of buildings that pushes the poor out
of place? In some passionate urban congregations the rebellion of the
Spirit against such a marring of the image of God in us is expressed
through shouting and noise. The leader's exhortation, 'Let us hear it in
the House!', is followed by yelling and whooping and ecstatic Halleluias.
Likewise, they exalt in the miraculous transformations for those lifted
out of their imprisonment of spirit. Both the yelling and the exhaltation
seem to give voice to the Spirit's yearning for change and release.

And yet, after all the noise and hope, things largely stay as they are.

Jim Wallis, the leader of the Sojourner movement in the USA, repeatedly defines faith as holding to the vision and working for the kingdom in the face of the evidence, and holding to that vision until the evidence changes! I warm to that sentiment, but we must reflect on the fact that for the vast majority of the faithful, the oppression has remained just the same for untold generations despite their pleading prayers to the Spirit of God to intervene. What does God make of that? If God's miracles occur only for the few and not always for the most faithful, could it be that the Holy Spirit is more like Jesus than we like to acknowledge? Maybe, just as Jesus suffered, so the Spirit suffers too and has determined that flames of fire will not descend from the skies, nor hosts of angels come to put things right (Luke 9.54–55; Matthew 26.53–54). Could it be that the Holy Spirit is as poor as Christ? Perhaps the Spirit truly shares the alienated, unacknowledged and rebuked nature of Jesus? Perhaps the truth is that the Holy Spirit has chosen to share Christ's alienation and powerlessness? Why should the Holy Spirit be different in character and intention from Jesus? Does not the nature of God make it unlikely, if not impossible, to gainsay the basic perimeters of creation and freewill which the Father has created for our good?

Physicality and the Holy Spirit

Against such a suggestion that the Spirit may in relation to humanity adopt the same self-denying attitude as did Jesus, many urban Christians across the world, and especially those living in the ghettos, believe that the Spirit of God brings not a solidarity of powerlessness but, on the contrary, honours the true Christian with splendid and manifest prosperity! When poor people are promised 'good news', why should they not legitimately expect it to entail riches and an escape from the thrall of poverty? When white missionaries first arrived in Africa, the populace was taken aback by the missionaries' lack of bodily awareness. They were offering a somewhat abstracted and cerebral faith rather than a holistic and down-to-earth one. So today, African and Hispanic urban Christians often major on the physicality of the renewing Spirit, revelling in the promise of the resurrection of the body as it may be even now experienced. It is assumed that spiritual renewal can therefore be anticipated in 'prosperity' as well as in 'well-being'. Prosperity often presents itself in the very high quality dress and general turn-out of the congregational leadership where those who have been restored through faith experience the Holy Spirit providing them with congregational or community power and a self-evident prosperity. They sense that if one is right with God, then God in turn is going to reward and bless the faithful with wealth and prosperity – and the evidence in turn helps those aspiring to faith to see that it must be a better and more physically beneficial way of life. Bling is powerful proof of God's desires for his children.

This sense of the importance to God of physicality leads some black London east-end congregations to prompt hundreds of their members to engage in a lively ministry of physical restoration in their urban communities – fighting gun-crime, drug trafficking and prostitution – as expressive of a realizable spirituality of renewal and redemption, and a counter-balance to their community's despised status. They see this drive to physicality as a gift of the Holy Spirit rather than in terms of an incarnational imperative.

Urban spirituality?

In the book *God in the City* (1995), I wrote a chapter entitled 'The Body: Physicality in the Urban Priority Area', in which I sought to show that a spiritual concern for the physical realities of life have high priority for urban people. There is an earnest desire for self-confidence and control, commitment and physical transcendence. That chapter was written in 1994, well before the latest arrivals of the new African ethnicities to our British cities. I suspect therefore that what I have written here about the importance of the physical realities of life as of deep spiritual concern is a description of something that is more culturally urban than ethnically generated. This assumption is reinforced when we compare the characteristics of the British nineteenth-century urban catholic movement (served by the so-called 'slum priests') with those of our contemporary urban charismatic scene. Both have taken delight in evocative symbolism and story, revelled in socially stimulating music and visual stimulus; both have enjoyed being somewhat out of the ordinary and a little suspect against the mainstream culture; both have wanted to 'do it right' in opposition to those who do not have the right esoteric doctrine, style or charism. It would seem right therefore to say that there is something which is specifically urban here and not simply ethnically engendered.

Spiritual praise

What differentiates the appreciation of physicality which urban Christians have from that of the prevailing, aggressively physical, culture of the urban scene is that the former is refined in the fire of Other-centred worship. My fellow contributors to *God in the City*, David Ford and Al McFadyen, stated in their chapter on 'Praise' that worship is not only 'essential for celebrating the heart of faith. It is also vital for enabling personal (and communal) dignity and identity and judging what is right and wrong (and why it is so)' (1995: 95). Open-eyed urban worship is joyful in the face of the harsh facts of life, and it opens us up in amazement before God's commitment to his children, so that we imagine everything for what it could become rather than what it presently is. In it we learn to refer everything to an Other who is ultimate, so that we are properly suspicious of anything around us which seeks to contradict that Other. Put simply, being in awe of God as we worship transforms us so radically that we begin to see ourselves truthfully, and are charged with energy to seek to transform the world around so that it might reflect the beauty of the God who made it.

Worship can unmask the pretence of both who we are and how the world should work. The myth is that the world can only work through aggressive competition one with another, but worship opens us to different truths. That the world must always be bleak and chaotic is, for the worshipper, no longer a given. That all things are now possible becomes self-evident. And as worship offers us new vision, putting harsh realities into a new light, so also the Spirit of worship empowers us to work for the beautiful in the face of ugliness. The ugliness is now seen for the sin that it is, as the Holy Spirit draws us together in worshipful solidarity so that we can make common cause against it. And in this very solidarity (*koinonia*) is a reaffirmation of our being as made in the image of the Holy Trinity and of the power which the Holy Spirit imparts. It is, however, a solidarity unlike that engendered by most political fervour, in that every individual counts within it – no matter how trivial and unlikely they may seem to 'the world'. The Holy Spirit constantly affirms the small and insignificant as loved by God.

This Spirit-filled hope is born of a true discernment of reality and is not deluded. It is open-eyed because the urban poor are the truth-tellers in our midst – their presence will not allow us to pretend about the quality of our society. There is therefore scant spiritual discernment without listening to the experience of the oppressed, and there is therefore great danger in formulating any theology away from the poor.

Space, place and the Holy Spirit

Having said that, we know too that not every urban congregation is a place where we find truth. Indeed, some churches are obviously used as places of escape from the world of urban reality, especially by those who believe that the Holy Spirit can be contained within the supernatural sphere. The abundance of monocultural churches (many based on ethnicity or socio-economy) is surely a flight from the surrounding diversity. Such churches will find support for their social isolation from within the Hebrew Scriptures which seem, on the face of it, intent on affirming the domination of one culture – the Jewish culture – over those surrounding it. But on the contrary, the New Testament story of Pentecost (Acts 2) demonstrates that with the coming of the Holy Spirit something quite different is afoot – the inclusion of cultures rather than their exclusion from grace. At Pentecost, the urban is the place God chooses for the Spirit's transformatory coming, for the city epitomizes the illusion of human self-sufficiency and aggrandizement. Just as the old myth of the Tower of Babel signified how humanity seeks in the city to show off its egotistical prowess and competitiveness, issuing in the monolithic uni-culture of the Tower, so the Spirit comes to affirm the mixity and cosmopolitan nature of the kingdom of God – for now all the nations could hear the truth in their own particular, cultural language. It is the presence of the Holy Spirit which allows each to hear the Good News in our own accent while the accent of the person next to us in the crowded city is affirmed with equal, divine passion.

This affirmation of the many and the mixity does not, however, ignore the intense particularity of the local person. The local accent and the local patch can still be real and affirmed – and not in the superficial way we have seen in recent times when the Irish, Cockney and Scouse cultures of the poor are 'used' as themes for pubs, TV soaps or theme parks. For despite the fact that many an urban locality can be alienating, those who live there may still want to refer to it as 'our turf', or 'my home town'. This speaks movingly of the fundamental human need for belonging and solidarity which is rooted in our being made in the image of the

Holy Trinity. Each person of the Trinity can be named only in relation to another person – the Son can only be such because there is the Father. So with humankind, they need others to find their own identity. In this search for belonging somewhere, each place can become Holy Ground, or as Brueggemann would have it, barren space can become a treasured and hallowed place when the lives of those who have lived there are celebrated in the hearts of its present inhabitants (2002).

However, the picture is becoming more complex. For now many urban people live their lives in such mobile and transient conditions that they are forced to find ways of making the space between places of arrival, rather than only the places themselves, a hallowed and treasured entity. The constant commuting as the local shops and employment are depleted, and the breakdown of propinquity of family life prompts today's urban people to discover that the Holy Spirit lives also in the journeys and networks as well as in the holy places – and that helps us to see that God is indeed in everything and not only in those localities where we would normally celebrate the divine presence. We learn from this once again that we depend on God rather than God depending on our transitory recognition of God.

Urban space is very contested space, where land prices can be sky-high, where differing cultures vie for recognition, where developers come and go, having left their marks upon the landscape and upon communities. Therefore, urban people have to become adept at encountering and negotiating with others who have a different take on the urban space that they have to occupy together. Negotiated encounter with otherness is a skill that simply has to be learnt if one is to survive well in contested urban space, and if the city is to function without its conflicts disabling its patterned life. Urban Christians therefore are able to come with experience and aptitude to an even greater encounter. For the Christian, wherever they may be, must risk the even greater encounter that is with the Ultimate Other – and they must learn that it is in that very encounter with the Holy Spirit of God that we change, grow and become more who we have it in us to be. Our selfhood remains provisional and always in a state of becoming, as it readies itself for its next encounter and negotiation. It is in the encounter with the Other (a daily urban event) that our Christian identity is forged. Urban Christians learn how to engage that Other by virtue of their everyday experience in their contested environment and are therefore more ready for that ultimate engagement – and perhaps are eager for it. I suspect that this is why urban theology has become the touchstone for the theology of the globalization that has more recently impacted upon the Church with all its challenge of mixity and cultural diversity.

Staying in the city?

So where, then, would I go to make spiritual retreat? Would I choose the countryside, where the Spirit can whisper in the wind across the fields, or should I turn my face to the city or the housing estate and see the tears of Jesus in the face of the old woman in the market? In Britain it is largely the urban which defines our individual identity since the vast majority of us (about 80 per cent) live in built-up areas, and those who don't actually live in urban areas watch a TV which is subtly pushing urban values at viewers even in its wildlife travelogues! As it is said, 'We are all urban now.' And does the Holy Spirit deplore that or relish it?

Jesus of course did not choose to begin his ministry in the cities of Galilee but initially aimed his mission particularly at the villages, and he did that for strong cultural and political reasons. He addressed the oppressed and militant villagers by appealing to the very radical 'Lesser Traditions' of the peasant people of the villages, thus attacking the prestigious elitist Greater Tradition of the religious aristocracy, protected in their cities. One has to remember that in the time of Jesus there was no Old Testament as we know it. There were instead the scattered Traditions, some written and many oral, from which only later were selected the Traditions that now make up our Old Testament (or 'Hebrew Scriptures'). We note that he chooses to minister first where the more radical parts of the tradition were most admired – the poor villages. Jesus aims his mission carefully at the capital city only when the time is right for him to do so. But even there he maintains the same strategy of turning the more radical 'Lesser Traditions' of the villages against those of the dominating powers of the elite. Inevitably he goes ultimately to the city, the seat of the power-elite, to engage in the final conflict and his ultimate victory.

In readiness for that victory, he tells his apprenticed disciples to 'stay in the city until you have been clothed with power from on high' (Luke 24.49). While in the city they must be expectant and no less than vigilant, in order to discern the Spirit when it comes upon them in power.

Therefore we, with them, must adopt a similar 'hermeneutical suspicion of spaces', as Kathryn Tanner (2004) puts it, and by the guiding discernment of the Holy Spirit uncover the power dynamics and cultural biases of our urban predicament. For it is here that we will find God heavily embedded, and where that superabundance of grace, of which I spoke earlier, will be realized. The city or housing estate will remain a complex arena where, despite its pending Pentecostal transformation from Old to New Jerusalem, still heaves with all its urban terrors of obsessive wealth and marginalized powerlessness. We must, as we are bidden by Jesus, wait to be clothed with the power from on high, but for most, the city will remain a prison where the Spirit is confined alongside the oppressed and where many know they are going nowhere. But the fervent desire of the Spirit is that the powers of hell in the city will be crushed so that the image of the loving and self-giving God may be seen afresh in creation. This same Spirit breaks in to our experience time and again – and as we glimpse it, as we encounter the Other, we are given power to break barriers and look on in awe of God's urban miracle.

Chapter 10

Bring and Share: The Urban Eucharist

MANDY FORD

The particularity of the Eucharist

A few years ago I was working with a small group from my church on a presentation for a conference of urban churches. At that time I was the curate in a parish in the heart of multicultural Leicester where we rejoiced in neighbours from all over the Indian sub-continent, most of whom were practising Hindus. At the conference we wanted to speak about our experience of being Christians in the city. At first our conversation centred on the familiar cultural and moral aspects of faith – the things which most people think of when they tick the box for 'Christian' on the census form. However, we realized that these aspects were not distinctive. We had recently shared a service with an Asian Christian group who began their service by lighting a ghee lamp, sang ragas rather than hymns, and finished with a lively stick-dance which we recognized as looking a lot like the rice-threshing dances with which our local Hindus celebrate Navatri (the Hindu 'harvest festival'). After this experience we could not express our Christianity in the terms of our liturgy or our church building, in our hymns or summer fetes. Similarly, we knew from experience that living a moral life is not distinctive to Christian faith. The Hindus, Sikhs and Muslims living around us were moral people, striving to live within their own religious codes, and indeed we were well aware of their kindness as good neighbours. What, we wondered, was distinctive for us? The answer, we decided, was the Eucharist. This was the thing that we did, every day in our parish, which gave us our identity and proclaimed the presence of God in the city.

I make no apology for our conclusion. I was working in a catholic parish where the balance between word and sacrament was weighted in favour of the latter. As has often been the case in deprived inner-city settings, the gospel was preached in action, in symbol and in liturgy more easily than in words. Elsewhere in this book Peter Robinson has written about proclamation in the city, and everything I write here should be read in tandem with his thoughts as we unfold the same gospel through sacrament and word.

This reference to proclamation is a reminder that both word and sacrament, proclamation and liturgy, involve a hermeneutic process through which texts and actions are interpreted in the light of our experience (see Vanhoozer et al.: 2007). The hermeneutic process helps us to move beyond systematic theology to the 'little theologies' shaped in local, in this case, urban contexts (Sedmak 2002). I have taken these things – the need for interpretation and the shaping of little theologies – as the starting point for my exploration of the urban Eucharist. The action of taking, blessing, breaking and sharing bread in remembrance of Jesus takes place in churches in cities in many different ways according to theology and tradition, and whether we call it the Lord's Supper and share a crumbled roll to the sound of a worship group or call it Mass and distribute the host in a cloud of incense, the urban setting also influences our understanding of these actions.

How do urban people read and receive the Eucharist? What experiences do they bring to the foundational meal of the Church which enables them to interpret it?

Bring and share

There is another meal which plays a significant part in the life of urban churches and which may help us to see the Eucharist in the urban afresh. This is the phenomenon of the 'Bring and share'. Every urban church I have ever worked in, or visited, is proud of the quality of its 'Bring and share'. This method of providing for a shared meal is quite particular to church life, and perhaps even more particular to urban church life. A 'Bring and share' is a community meal with some special characteristics.

A 'Bring and share' is nearly always suggested by the congregation and not by the vicar. A call goes out; perhaps a note in the weekly notice-sheet, to alert everyone to the occasion, and no further planning is needed. Occasionally someone may have suggested writing a list of items required for the meal, but this is generally disregarded by those who bring the food. The church hall is set out with plastic tables and chairs, paper plates and serviettes. There will be one or two large tables for the food and there may be smaller tables or card tables for those who need to sit to eat. On the day of the meal, people bring their food offerings in carrier bags and plastic boxes, in cake tins and cling-filmed bowls. There may be some 'gate-keepers' – ladies who take the offerings and plate them up – but they never reject what is brought. We hope that no one has brought anything too weird, but this cannot be guaranteed in a multicultural congregation. If there are Caribbean members there may be rice and peas, or goat curry and dumplings. Our Asian friends will bring home-made samosas and spicy fried chicken to set alongside the fairy cakes and meat-paste sandwiches. There will be piles of sausage rolls and bought snacks and packet cakes too. It will be simple food, there is no showing off, and no one likes to stand out in this crowd or look like they have been 'cheffy'.

People will pile their plates and sit at tables or graze while standing up. Food may be eaten in any order. There may be wine or juice to drink, but there will also be cups of tea or coffee – almost certainly served in that pale blue or green china which lurks in the cupboards in every church hall and community centre. And if you only wandered into church this morning, or you did not read the news-sheet, or you cannot afford to bring anything at all, you are still welcome to stay and share the meal. During the meal, stories will be told; the 'Bring and share' is often an opportunity to impart church history, recalling significant occasions or similar meals: the time when Father Terry bought mince pies for everyone, or an ice-cream van drew up in the car park.

At the end of the meal everyone helps to clear up, wash up the cups, sweep the floor and stack the chairs. They take pride in the fact that there is always plenty left over, and it will be bagged up and pressed into the hands of the neediest, the young families and the asylum-seekers, before everyone goes home.

Putting on a good 'Bring and share' gives the church community a sense of pride. People who are individually reticent are collectively welcoming. People who are individually economically challenged are collectively generous. People who are individually unsure of their role in society find a collective identity in the church.

The wedding banquet

The 'Bring and share' is the wedding banquet of the urban church. It is the context in which we understand the Eucharist as part of the continuity of meals we share together. Joachim Jeremias has commented that the same is true for our understanding of the Last Supper, as 'In reality, the "founding meal" is only one link in a long chain of meals which Jesus shared with his followers and which they continued after Easter . . . the Last Supper has its historical roots in this chain of gatherings' (quoted in Peterson 2005: 214). If we interpret the 'Bring and share' within the chain of meals which Jesus shared, we recognize the culture of hospitality which turns normal rules upside down and in which generosity is always sufficient – sometimes seemingly by divine providence!

A 'Bring and share' is a meal at which those on the edge of the church community find the easiest welcome and are most comfortable. The folks who do not have a family and a Sunday lunch to go home to are delighted, like the poor, the crippled, the lame and the blind, to enjoy the wedding feast rejected by those originally invited. When the regular churchgoers rush off, there always seem to be plenty of others to enjoy the food. A share in the meal does not demand any reciprocity; it is an invitation to those who cannot repay as well as those who can (Luke 14.1–14).

As the food arrives, people often draw a parallel between the 'Bring and share' and the feeding of the five thousand. We are never sure that there will be enough, but there always seems to be more than sufficient, and plenty left over. There is a sense of God's provision, in which food which may be scarce at home, and which is not necessarily healthy or of 'good quality', is transformed into a feast by its abundance, variety and the context of celebration (John 6.1–14).

However, the food of the Eucharist is not only transformed but retains its character as the fragile produce of human economy which is deeply implicated in human sin. This point is powerfully made by Geoffrey Preston, quoted by Timothy Radcliffe in *Why Go to Church*:

> Think of the dominations, exploitation and pollution of man and nature that goes with bread [. . .] all the wicked oddity of a world distribution that brings plenty to some and malnutrition to others, bringing them to that symbol of poverty we call the breadline. And

wine too [...] the sources of some of the most tragic forms of human degradation: drunkenness, broken homes, sensuality, debt. What Christ bodies himself into is bread and wine like this. (2008: 103)

When we bring the food to the altar, or to the 'Bring and share' table, we know that what we bring is inadequate and poor; we do not hide the reality of our lives nor our complicity in the economics of mass production and distribution. For my congregation these things are unavoidable as our church is located on the edge of a shopping precinct in the shadow of a superstore. But for every urban congregation, whether at a 'Bring and share' or a harvest festival, the food arrives in a selection of carrier bags, each bearing its badge of shame, its supermarket logo.

The eucharistic community

Where there is coherence between the gospel, the Eucharist and the culture of the 'Bring and share', they act together as a critique of the city as a place of injustice and atomization. Whereas life beyond the church walls may be atomized, unjust and inhospitable, what our practice proclaims is the unifying, just and hospitable love of God. The relationship between food and proclamation is not accidental; Jesus used meals as an opportunity to share the good news of God's love, and there are more than ten meals alluded to in the Gospel of Luke alone. At its simplest level, a shared meal recollects those biblical meals and helps to make Jesus present among us. Both the 'Bring and share' and the Eucharist create a space in which unity is revealed in difference, in which relationships are not transactional but defined by the economy of the gift and in which the grace of God is expressed in love, service and hospitality.

The 'Bring and share' is a cultural phenomenon which stands in stark contrast to that other cultural phenomenon, the middle-class dinner party. The culture of the dinner party expresses the aspirational and transactional nature of food, not only as a social substance that binds relationships together but social *currency* expressing power within relationships. What is bought, cooked and served expresses the hosts' standing in society and that of their guests. The food will be cooked by a single person, using recipes from well-known chefs, there will be a series of courses, served on the best china, surrounded by flowers and candles, and everyone will be on their best behaviour. At its worst this is privatized, competitive and transactional activity – everything the Eucharist is not.

If the 'Bring and share' stands in opposition to the middle-class dinner party, it is also counter-cultural in poorer communities where increasingly privatized social space and smaller families have led to a marked decline in the casual 'dropping-in' culture which was still prevalent in working-class communities when Michael Northcott was writing about urban culture in 1998 (Northcott 1998). It is no longer common for people to eat together, either in social or family settings, except on celebratory occasions. This reality gives every shared meal a celebratory atmosphere.

However, if the Eucharist can be read as a counter-cultural expression of the gospel, it questions our liturgical and ecclesial practice. What do the people who share so happily in the meal *after* our worship make of the meal that takes place *within* our worship? How are they interpreting it?

Whatever the appearance of our celebration of the Eucharist, our liturgical and ecclesiastical practice retains the character of a cultic meal with its roots in the Jewish Passover. Participation in the meal not only brings the community together, it defines the community, and more significantly it defines membership of the community. Church discipline insists that we do not simply offer bread and wine to anyone who walks through the door. In reality our Eucharistic practice shows that we are still concerned with who belongs to the body of Christ and who does not. We are still vulnerable to our human desire for identity, and to the sin which insists on defining our identity in opposition to the 'other'. Whatever we say, our eucharistic practice is not all-inclusive.[1] As the congregation lines up to receive Communion, or gathers around the altar, there will be some who are denied the sacrament: the youngest, the unknown visitor, the new arrival who is preparing for Confirmation. Is it clear to these brothers and sisters of Christ that they are sharing in the Eucharist? This is a question which has become heightened in the light of recent anxieties around the 'swine flu' pandemic, when once again some congregations have been faced with sharing a Eucharist in one kind while the presiding minister alone consumes the wine. Whatever our theology, perhaps we should be more rigorous in asking how our actions are interpreted. For, as Steven Shakespeare and Hugh Rayment-Pickard have written: 'Jesus is the kingdom in action, for all that we want to fix his essence in doctrines and structures. In the end, Jesus did not say "Believe this" or "Know this" or "Submit to this in memory of me". He said "*Do* this in memory of me." And then he fed his friends' (Shakespeare and Rayment-Pickard 2006: 99).

The challenge of the Eucharist

The theology of the 'Bring and share' challenges the Church to live out the gospel values of the priesthood of all believers in its eucharistic practice (1 Peter 2.5–9). Perhaps we need to be challenged, like those first-century residents of Corinth, to remember that the Eucharist is not simply another cultic occasion, but rather one which is intended to transform us and reveal our unity, not define it (1 Corinthians 10.16).

Those who preside over the Eucharist are vulnerable not only to the desire for control but the desire for excellence, which as I have already pointed out, is the opposite of the character of the 'Bring and share'. The feast may be very good, but it will undoubtedly lack the elegance, subtlety or craft of a well-prepared buffet. The poverty of the feast is transformed by the grace of God.

Kester Brewin has written eloquently on worship in the emergent church in which the gifts of the people can be brought and shared. He stresses the importance of the genuine gift, the gift which is true to the identity of the giver, the gift which has integrity and the gift which is indigenous to its locality. Such a gift is not valued according to its material worth, or even to the quality it brings to worship, but for itself. Such a gift cannot be bought, neither can it be 'bought in' (Brewin 2004: 117ff).

It takes generosity and love for the Church to receive these gifts as contributions to its liturgy. The music group that is always a little off-key, the intercessions that go on and on, the nervous reader who cannot really be heard and the servers wearing track-shoes under their ill-fitting albs, are never going to fit the urban church for a slot on *Songs of Praise*. But, as Timothy Radcliffe (2008) gently reminds us, God gives us dignity by allowing us to offer things to him, our inadequate worship, our taste-less white wafers, ourselves.

Placing the breaking of bread in the context of worship reminds us that the Eucharist is a complete offering of thanksgiving which is only completed by the whole community. As the priest stands in the centre of that community, holding the elements in her hands, it is as if there is an ever-expanding ripple of meaning. The chalice is the presence of Christ at the heart of a worshipping community which is the presence of Christ at the heart of its neighbourhood.

And at the end of the meal, the fragments are shared out and taken out into the neighbourhood.

Scattering the fragments

At the beginning of this exploration I suggested that the communal meals of the Church, whether the Eucharist or the 'Bring and share', were a counter-cultural critique of the society in which they are set. My final challenge is to ask whether this critique has any real resonance once Sunday morning is over and the fragments are scattered in the wider community. How do we remember the self-giving of Christ, the blood shed once for all for our sins, made present in our midst and effective in our lives?

I believe that we remember because we are able to express gratitude, and our gratitude is expressed in self-giving. Many of the traditional resonances of the Eucharist are harder to hear or see in the urban context. When many of us do not work, it is hard to feel any sense of solidarity with those who turn wheat into bread by 'the work of human hands' and to join in the offering of human endeavour in the physical elements of the Eucharist. When many of us do not earn, we have a different relationship with the money which is offered at the table, and it is hard to see it as an expression of our worth being offered to God. We are already broken people, so that the breaking of the body of Christ seems to be in solidarity with us as much as an offering for us. Because of this, we have a stronger sense of our offering being an offering of ourselves, broken as we already are, to be formed and shaped into the body of Christ.

Personally, the most powerful experience of presiding at the Eucharist has been the experience of being formed and shaped by the people around me and recognizing that I am not able to act 'in persona Christi' alone but only as one of the worshipping community. My prayers, my theology degrees, my ordination, are not sufficient unless they are joined with those of the treasures of the church who make up our congregation. I have learned hospitality at the altar.

Does the eucharistic community learn to offer hospitality beyond the walls of the church building? My own experience and the anecdotal evidence of urban churches around Britain suggest that it does. Our small church has consistently offered a place of companionship (the sharing of bread and friendship) to asylum-seekers and refugees. A group of older church members meet together each week intentionally providing a setting into which other isolated older people receive hospitality and cake! We gradually grow in confidence to offer hospitality beyond the confines of the eucharistic setting, although for practical reasons that hospitality is often offered within the church building. Eugene Peterson, among others, has pondered whether we have diminished our opportunities for evangelism in the modern world as we have marginalized hospitality (Peterson 2005: 215). Christ's hospitality challenges us both in our churches and in our homes. Just as the hospitality of the 'Bring and share' reflects our understanding of the gospel, so the gospel challenges us to take our 'Bring and share' hospitality beyond the walls of the church.[2]

Part 5

Engaging

FOUR CASE STUDIES

Eden Fitton Hill: Demonstrating and Becoming in Oldham

ANNA THOMPSON

Your attitude should be the same as that of Christ Jesus . . .

Eden Fitton Hill is a part of the Eden Network, a family of missional communities initiated in Greater Manchester but now spreading across the north. Eden began in 1997 in response to the realization that to enable young people in Britain's toughest communities to encounter Christian faith and flourish in discipleship, a new approach was needed. Eden in Fitton Hill began in 2003 in partnership with the Salvation Army's NEO network with a church plant and a team of people committed to learning what Church in Fitton Hill might look like.

Fitton Hill is a large housing estate just south of Oldham town centre; it struggles with multiple deprivations and a history of racial violence. Fitton Hill might be regarded as the 'not quite urban'; while it is classified as urban in a broad sense, it is literally on the margins and a world away from the choice-driven, energetic culture of the city.

In considering our focus on urban ministry, Eden is also inspired by Andrew Grinnell's language of the 'Forgotten 5%' – those places that are genuinely marginalized in our nation and, perhaps even more pointedly, largely forgotten by the Church. These communities provoke a question that deserves an answer: has God forgotten? We believe that in the heart of the *missio dei* there is an injunction to every believer to be sent, carrying God into the lives of the 'not quite included'.

'Who, being in very nature God, did not consider equality with God something to be grasped . . .'

At the heart of Eden is incarnation; we follow Christ as he 'became flesh and blood and moved into the neighbourhood'. Chris Neilson, the leader of Eden Fitton Hill, initiated the project, having spent three years already rooted in the Eden ethos in another part of the city. He recognizes that up until that point his understanding of incarnation equated to being 'like' his community, identifying with its customs and rituals. In Fitton Hill the penny dropped, *the sacrifice of the incarnation was its real power*. Creating common culture will be fruitless without the presence of real equality. Chris articulates: 'Church can be like a party; you come in and there's a cool crowd in the middle of the lounge having fun, you take your place by the buffet and wait until it's time to go home because you're not included.' The sacrifice of the incarnation means that the people who come in for the first time become the centre of the party.

' . . . but made himself nothing, taking the very nature of a servant, being made in human likeness . . .'

Entering into the incarnation of Christ in a new community involves an emptying, a stripping away. At times people have engaged in Eden teams believing that they can layer the new culture of their community on top of their inherited cultural leanings. These people work hard,

embracing customs and cultural habits. However, incarnation is not a job description, it is a life – and a task-focused approach to culture results in tired, fragmented individuals who yearn to 'relax and be themselves' in their familiar cultural surroundings. The kenosis of incarnation demands that cultural defaults are consciously surrendered in favour of sharing life with a new community. Only then can sustainable, authentic ministry be undertaken in a community without paternalism, and only then can the community itself become empowered. Skills and knowledge can be shared mutually without defences when cultural differences are removed. Fitton Hill is home.

'. . . *and being found in appearance as a man, he humbled himself and became obedient to death – even death on a cross!*'

During the early years, this process of self-emptying enabled the Eden team to reimagine what Church in Fitton Hill might look like. In Eden, Christian faith and Fitton Hill meet and are introduced to one another. The team come knowing something of God but needing to learn about the estate – and the estate knows itself but has more to learn of following Jesus: being Church in this place is going to have to be a partnership. Beginning with their only commonality, eating together, Eden Fitton Hill began to express gathered Church in their community; this soon became having a laugh together with food, silly games and prayer. For the team this became a cycle of *demonstrating* faith and *becoming* Fitton Hill; the young people involved found themselves *demonstrating* Fitton Hill and *becoming* full of renewed hope through faith in Christ. Chris acknowledges that 'in effect it meant asking new people to do stuff in the service'; and the team began to be mentored by the kids of Fitton Hill, who showed them how Fitton Hill did life, social events and worship. As a result of this empowering approach the church community attracted leaders: kids and adults who were natural influencers and who were given the opportunity to be involved quickly and simply – cooking, washing up, organizing events, playing music, praying in a gathering.

'Therefore God exalted him to the highest place and gave him the name that is above every name, that at the name of Jesus every knee should bow, in heaven and on earth and under the earth, and every tongue confess that Jesus Christ is Lord, to the glory of God the Father'

As Eden Fitton Hill has journeyed over the last five years its understanding of its mission has also evolved. Community transformation

has become the vision and purpose driving the church, gathering up kingdom values and focusing them on Fitton Hill. The church community continues to grow as people increasingly articulate faith in Jesus. However, Chris maintains that not only is the progress of Eden not dependent on Sunday attendance but it centres on serving the needs of the whole community of Fitton Hill, not just those who will respond to a personal call to faith in Christ. This means considering creating structures that make Fitton Hill work better, and in keeping with Eden's commitment to holistic practice, Chris and his wife Laura have initiated Hope Citadel, a proposal for an integrated health and community centre linking a surgery, dentist, library and community space for the youth service and other agencies to use, with a central reception and a joined-up approach. In the cycle of demonstrating and becoming, Laura and Chris now exercise leadership in drawing both agencies and the community together to see this dream fulfilled. As they are now themselves indigenous, their skills become part of Fitton Hill's social capital and the community recognize them as their own, enabling vital positive connections with government and community agencies.

Success for Eden in Fitton Hill involves both personal and social transformation. It is a growing body of people for whom faith in Jesus is a real and defining element of life, and who are sowing seeds of the kingdom within the wider community of Fitton Hill. It is seeing the people of the estate flourish so that Fitton Hill knows itself to be no longer forgotten but a cherished and fruitful community, together articulating hope for its future.

St Jude's, Earl's Court: The Hum to Touch the Heart

TOM GILLUM

'Church to become centre for poor and needy residents.' So read the head-line of *Garden Square News* (Autumn 2004). A photo of St Jude's Church, Courtfield Gardens in London's Earl's Court gave colour to the lead story. 'It's a lovely old church and we are all very sorry that it's not going to be a normal church' one resident was quoted as saying. The reaction of others I was talking with at the same time was more along the lines of, 'The poor and needy: isn't that what the Church is meant to be doing anyway?'

As I now read what I am quoted as having said, it is a bit vague and general. Community of St Jude (CSJ), a 'Fresh Expression', has lived with the uncertainty that our identity and direction would only become clear as time passes. The Community of Sant' Egidio in Rome[1] was our initial inspiration. When I first read about this European movement, I warmed to their approach. Others were also exploring how to 'anglicize' what had begun in 1968, in the aftermath of Vatican II.

My wife Joanna and I met with some of their leaders in 2001. Claudio Betti charmed us over coffee and Campari, told stories, and we found our hearts being touched. It was simple, prayerful, highly rela-tional – and they preached the gospel (which drew the evangelical in me). He urged us to get going. 'What's your model?' I asked him. I cannot repeat his answer; but he wanted me to know Sant' Egidio was 'an experience, not a model'. We wondered what he meant by that.

Here was a successful marrying of spirituality with social action, two sides of the same coin. Attempts by some to do a 'transplant' in England were not proving sustainable (few Britons can pronounce Sant' Egidio!) We were in London, not Rome, with our climate and a

125

different church context, but we could start by gathering people to pray with us and getting to know 'the poor and needy' in Earl's Court.

Christianity, brought to life for me through evangelicalism, has always been located in a 'personal relationship'. Descriptive of both our communion with God and fellowship within the Church (and increasingly seen as central for effective evangelism), a joining of heart and mind was 'what it is about'. Doubtless helped by the beauty of Rome and the charm of the Italians, we saw 'personal relationship' unselfconsciously taken to include 'the poor' – in friendship. The bonds of 'community' were as evident between the members as they were with 'the poor'.

Evangelicals have a long history of recognizing the importance of 'mercy ministries'. Cautious about going too far down a road which might dilute the supremacy of grace by a hefty dose of 'good works', such ministries are seen as acts of service and obedience, with 'providers' and 'receivers'. At the same time, prayer is of central importance to evangelicals, a main expression of our relationship with God. Much of it happens alone and perhaps we assume more than is actually the case. The clear message from Sant' Egidio was that through friendship with the poor, God uniquely reveals to us his heart; prayer and social action are inseparable.

Four years on from the *Garden Square News* article, at the initiative of the Bishop of London we held the first CSJ Congress. There was a remarkable sense of 'community' and it was fascinating to hear how lives had been touched.

Experiences of 'natural, organic relations', 'something grounded', 'a simplicity of word and action' and 'helping me to live in the present for God' were described. It was appreciated that 'the Bible is not rammed down your throat'. Our Visitor, Adrian Chatfield, spoke of a 'hum which had touched his heart'. Looking round the room, many present had not met before. But that they were connected as 'CSJ' was without doubt. It was a remarkably strong bond, and the little we and they have done seems to have gone a remarkably long way. Belonging means being joined in a net, where a little praying and working together provide the key points of contact, fostered by food, hospitality and simple articulation of our life in a fortnightly newsletter.

There are now 27 members. Quite a number of others, however (the edges are blurred) join in our rhythm of prayer or with us as we befriend those easily forgotten and ignored behind often impressive (and surprisingly inaccessible) urban facades. Praying with us, for most, means either coming to an open small group which meets twice a week for half an hour, or meeting with a few others in a home to pray before going to work; or for fifteen minutes of mainly silent prayer at St Jude's Church. Those we befriend include the elderly, the homeless and bedsit residents, prisoners, and, in the pipeline, asylum-seekers and local sex workers.

Friendship may be the best word we have, but it may need some reclamation to do justice to the true meaning of 'loving our neighbour'. What better place to start than the Trinity where lies central relationship, enjoyed for its own sake. In time-poor, money-rich London, spending an hour with a woman in the twilight of her life or with a man in a Night Shelter is good training for learning personal relationship – God's way. We may find we are in fact less skilled than we had thought in our relational ability. It may not come easily to start with someone else's agenda or to be willing to reveal myself and connect, heart to heart, without which we will never discover the deep connectedness we share as humans. All good training for prayer.

Human participation in the life of the Trinity reveals grace at its most sublime. It is 'personal relationship' with 'other'. The inseparable link between the two great commandments means that truly to 'know' God must also involve loving our neighbour – in the way shown by Jesus. In practice, at least in Earl's Court, this requires a proactive choice to cross a social, age or cultural divide. This big step is a commitment to Christ to live with the counter-cultural priority of being a friend of someone whose world we do not know. This is different from the institutionalization of social action, inbuilt in which is a relational imbalance that comes with hoping to 'help the poor and needy' – we may need to ask how much we really have helped.

Friendship with 'the poor' is not always easy to sustain, but doing so as part of a 'community' is both practical, usually more fun, and it is 'biblical'. The same principle applies to prayer. Without suggesting that it is the only thing, to pray is, for one of Jesus' followers, central and normative as an expression of 'loving God'. This is not just a 'private and personal' thing, where so many seem to get stuck. The reality for many in London is that regular prayer is beyond reach. Locating prayer in CSJ's rhythm, something beyond me and to which I have voluntarily chosen to submit, leads paradoxically to new confidence and delight in true participation in 'personal relationship' with the God and Father of Jesus Christ.

At the Congress, much was made of the atmosphere of CSJ being non-judgemental and low key. Members have, at a Service of Reception, declared their intent to participate in the rhythm of prayer. While goodwill is there, people overestimate what they can do. The 'hum to touch the heart' comes from the voluntary offering of a human life in response to the inviting grace of God in Christ, a choice to join in a life bigger than my own; the experience of the Trinity, not a model.

CSJ has identified the Body of Christ as its other central theological principle. For St Paul, this is more than just a metaphor, and I think he would see several members of CSJ gathering with a few elderly women in the lounge where they live, including visitors and staff who want to join in, as a chance to encounter the living Christ. In London, mission demands that we go out to gather people, where they are, wherever that is realistic, so that the gospel of the kingdom can be proclaimed and lived out.

We expect to hear Christ. Our reading of scripture is careful and attentive. *Lectio divina* and praying the Psalms (mainly silently) accompany Bible study and exposition. The dynamic of a seemingly spontaneous group (we seldom know who will be with us) 'colliding' in a meeting under the word of God is most creative and fruitful. What we have heard we allow to set the tone of our prayer. There is a breadth of ownership and accessibility of the Bible which leads to growing confidence of our equal participation in the Body of Christ. One of our members, a homeless man, captured what CSJ would aspire to be when he said, 'We have adopted each other, haven't we? We can go now and adopt others to join us.'

We expect to experience something of Christ's grace. On Friday evenings, a few gather for a simple healing liturgy. At the climax, all are invited to be anointed with oil, hands open to *receive Christ's healing touch to make us whole*. We all meet as 'poor and needy' creatures, under sin and death. We also proclaim that our humanity is being renewed now and we anticipate the fullness of Christ's redemption at the New Creation.

Mission must beat loud at the heart of the Church. Encouragingly, it has been non-church people who have tended to 'get it' quicker when we describe what we are trying to do. It seems to make sense that Christianity at heart is 'prayerful' and that it takes us to people 'on the edges of life'. The second is usually the easier initial point of contact. In these unexpected relationships, each has opportunity to see him- or herself in a new light, which in turn allows for repentance. The reality of what commitment to Christ may involve can be seen at close quarters. In twos and threes at home, at work, in the everyday of life (and not in an ecclesiastical building) strangers have begun to become a family, the new people of God.

Our aim is that in its structures, CSJ will show and draw all people to the core of the gospel. To quote T. S. Eliot, 'the end is where we start from'. This means an experience of Trinitarian community; grace-filled, very personal relationships.

St Aubyn's, Devonport:
Faith and the Quality of Life

DAVID NIXON

Introduction

The parish of St Aubyn, Devonport, on the west side of the city of
Plymouth, is almost exactly co-terminous with one of the 39 projects
under the banner of New Deals for Communities. This scheme brought
large amounts of investment from central government to some of the
most socially deprived neighbourhoods of England, not simply to
impose regeneration on local communities but actively to engage them
in the work of social change. The Devonport Regeneration Community
Partnership was given the task of spending £48.5 million during the
period 2001–11.

From the outset, faith issues were part of the mainstream of the
Partnership, with the Anglican Community priest who was resident
(though not licensed to the parish) as a member of the main Board,
and chair of a working group entitled Faith and Quality of Life, situated within the theme of Health: one of the five themes (Crime, Health
Education, Work and Environment) around which the regeneration
work was based. When this priest left her post, as the new incumbent I
became chair of the Faith group and was subsequently appointed as
Faith and Quality of Life representative on the Board, where I am
expected to continue until the end of the project.

This case study sets out to describe what happened and is happening
in Devonport in the interaction between Community Partnership and
local faith communities, and to analyse this in terms of a mission-
orientated church. The notion of faith communities includes here four
Christian denominations with three permanent buildings, most of
whose leaders (including myself) are non-resident. The local popula-

tion is predominantly white working class, with a tiny number of black and minority ethnic residents. Of these, some would be Christian and others Muslim. There was a larger Muslim population when Devonport was used for asylum-seekers' arrivals, but these numbers dropped considerably after dispersal through the city. As far as I am aware, there were never any formal worship meetings of Muslims in the area. Theologically, I come with the assumption that God is already present and at work in the world, and especially in vulnerable communities like St Aubyn's parish, through church bodies and secular agencies; and that our role is to discover God's presence, and co-create the transformation of human lives.

Events and activities

There are four areas of activity I wish to consider: the development of a Faith and Quality of Life Strategy and its implementation, work with the St Aubyn's congregation and the parish church, the removal of the Devonport Dockyard wall, and the implications for the local Anglican priest of being a Board member.

The Faith and Quality of Life Strategy was an attempt by the working group to express some of its discussions, aims and hopes in terms of a document which would follow the pattern of other Partnership strategies in setting out a case for action and delivery, and enabling these to be quantified and assessed. While attempting to define *faith* and *quality of life*, we recognized from the outset that this strategy would be more fuzzy than, for example, one which intended to raise GCSE passes or improve rates of coronary heart disease. Writing the strategy forced some simple research about the advantages of including faith communities in regeneration work and the difficulties they faced in such engagement. A requirement to describe the current faith and spiritual scene in Devonport led to a small-scale Spirituality Audit of church congregations and community groups, as well as community consultations recorded by video and written on a 'tablecloth'. Local people spoke about their hopes and fears in life, as well as their reflections on the local area. The Community Partnership funded a visit to Manchester, Leeds and Oldham to find out what faith groups in other similar areas were doing with their buildings, how they linked to community organizations, and what connection they had with statutory funding. These insights were distilled into the Faith and Quality of Life Strategy, and interpreted in terms of possibilities for Devonport.

The overall aim of the strategy was 'That people in Devonport will have access to excellent quality services, information, resources and support that will improve their quality of life and to celebrate freely their community and their part in it'. This was followed by three Priorities and further Strategic Aims, for example: Priority 1 – Faith and Spiritual Well-Being, Strategic Aim: 'To ensure that local people have access to spiritual and emotional support, spiritual space and the opportunity to join in all aspects of faith and spiritual well-being.' Key Objectives and Initial Actions were determined for each Priority, e.g. Information on religious and faith activities available to all; Spiritual Space identified and accessible to all; Celebrating religious festivals – faith communities to engage the community in celebration. A further paper about implementation described the distribution of these activities around the five key themes, with a committee called Community Accountability involved with overall monitoring. We used the concept of spiritual capital here, modelled on that of social capital, which we hoped to build in the regeneration process (for social capital in faith terms, see *Faith as Social Capital* from the Joseph Rowntree Foundation; for faithful capital or religious capital, see *Faithful Cities* from the Commission on Urban Life and Faith).

If there was occasionally the need to remind regeneration professionals that the churches represented valuable community groups, there was also teaching required for the mainly elderly congregation of St Aubyn's, that the regeneration work going on in their streets and their parish was not wholly different from the transformation of human lives in which we were engaged as a Christian community: that the resurrection of Jesus included new life now in Devonport, especially for the most vulnerable. A desire for openness, outwardness and generosity contrasted with the tendency towards a siege mentality, represented by the doors of the church being firmly closed at the start of a service (although traffic noise was always given as the primary explanation). In practical terms, the Community Partnership paid for refreshments after Carol Services and similar events on the grounds that these were moments of community celebration. The church building, for many years beyond the needs and means of the congregation, became a focus of change, firstly in envisaging the effect that different arrange-

ments of furniture had on eucharistic worship, and then in considering dual and alternative uses and their implications. At present the intention is to develop Devonport Library on the ground floor of the building, with a new mezzanine and repaired galleries forming a combined performance/worship space. The result would be a watertight building with new heating and lighting, open to the public most of the week, the conversion costs being met by the Partnership.

The church building was also used for gathering, shelter and a refreshment point at the moment when a large section of the Devonport Dockyard wall was knocked down. This three-metre wall topped with razor wire had split the north and south halves of Devonport since the 1950s, as the Navy expanded during the Cold War, contributing to the area a sense of exclusion and decay. This symbolic event of destruction, and the hope that it envisaged with a new shopping and residential centre in place of the grey lines of naval premises, took place immediately opposite St Aubyn's church, underscoring the church's central position in notions of regeneration, and perhaps convincing congregational doubters that they too were included.

Taking the role of Faith and Quality of Life Board Member has been an exciting, educative and challenging position. I should like to

mention three aspects of this role. Perhaps because of previous experience of university chaplaincy, there were moments of informal chaplaincy to the staff of the Partnership, ranging from social contacts, to
discussion about Board members who were difficult to work with, to
periodic briefings with the Chief Executive who enjoyed being questioned. The role was clearly perceived in a different light from those
occupied by either resident Board members, or the statutory representatives of health services, police or housing associations for example.
A second connected aspect related to the role during Board meetings.
Here I found a useful niche at awkward moments in reminding the
Board of the good work we were doing (and had done), and by inject-
ing humour to lighten the mood. When my appointment was reviewed
and I was asked to continue the role, one comment was that I acted
(whether I had chosen it or not) as 'the conscience of the Board'. A
third and final aspect is cautionary: such a role is not without its draw-
backs in terms of how the priest or parish is viewed. In Devonport,
during a particularly stormy period, the Board had to force the resigna-
tion of one of its members, behind whom was a small but vociferously
disgruntled group. With a few caveats which were discussed, I believed
that the Board was making the right decision, but this led to me being
positioned by some as 'one of them' rather than 'one of us', to posters
around the area condemning the decision and including references to
me individually, and for myself the uncomfortable feeling that my
usual support of the underdog had been undermined.

Analysis

These events, activities, positioning and possibilities require a very brief
critical consideration, leading perhaps to an enhanced understanding
of mission in an urban context. Two motifs employed by Myers (1994)
are echoed in this account – the first is that of centre and periphery, the
second that of entitlement. Helpfully, Myers operates these via the language of the built environment:

> The architecture of entitlement prevents us from encountering what
> is 'on the other side'. Yet if we are ever to be motivated to join Jesus in
> the deconstructive struggle, it will be because we have seen and been
> moved by the human faces of those condemned by the *locus imperii* to
> live on the other side of those walls (Myers, 1994: 202).

Myers understands the ministry of Jesus to be for the most part not at the metropolitan centre of Israel, but at its margins, both geographically and humanly speaking, suggesting that theology needs to move from the centre to the periphery, from the powerful to the less powerful. Within the Diocese of Exeter, St Aubyn's parish is peripheral on many reckonings: an inner-city area within a diocese which considers itself rural, on the far western boundaries of the diocese 50 miles from Exeter, on the western edges of the city of Plymouth, in the top five per cent nationally for indicators of deprivation. Almost like a photo-negative of Myers' image, architecture is one of the lenses through which to understand its history, culture and regeneration. The 'place of empire' where the power of the Royal Navy has until recently been centred is on the other side of the wall, which not only has cut a community in two, but also creates and separates places of participation and entitlement from places of exclusion and marginality. This enclave, while providing the city with much-needed employment, seems to have taken the lifeblood out of the community in which it is situated, so that Devonport since the 1950s has become almost literally dis-heartened. The images of the wall being breached are therefore hugely symbolic in drawing a line under the past, and providing hope for future entitlements.

The application of these motifs to the mission work of the church would look towards moves from centre to periphery, from an architecture of exclusion and marginality to one of inclusion and participation. This dynamic is reflected in the case study of St Aubyn's parish and its activities in relation to the Community Partnership. In this sense, the slightly mechanical and formulaic approach to regeneration has not hindered the work of urban mission; rather, the funding restrictions have forced the church to be really itself, rather than an inward-looking shadow of its own reality. The critical question is now to ask: Has the local church perhaps associated itself too closely with the formal regeneration funders, so that it fails to see where the regeneration does not upset inequity, or indeed adds to it?

A second significant question can be developed out of the theological assumption about God's pre-existence in the transformation of Devonport. We might ask: What has the church's involvement with the Partnership added? Or more topically: What is the church's Unique Selling Point here? The answer to these questions could be key to further work with national and local government agencies. A starting point for an answer lies in the notion of process mentioned above; human relations and human history are highly significant factors in regeneration, not simply extras to a plan for new streets and new buildings. These relations and history operate at the level of the local community as a whole (here in Devonport, through affluence, to war-time destruction, to post-war development, to slow decay) through to individuals in their context, familial and communal. The stories of the community intersect with the stories of particular lives to produce a whole range of human experience, from tragedy to comedy. At its best, Christianity has a long history of working with these sorts of stories, with these lived experiences of culture; indeed, Christian faith comes to its meanings through the vehicle of narrative, both human and divine. The Church's uniqueness therefore may lie in its ability to connect stories at all different levels, from multiple sources at varied times, and to affirm purpose and meaning in the human condition.

By asking what it would be like had the church not involved itself in this regeneration project, we see the way in which a dynamic of mission has operated internally. By opening itself to contact with a wider group of local residents than would otherwise have happened, as well as with staff members who are highly committed to welfare and

justice issues (though these would not often be couched in terms of faith) the church itself is potentially re-converted to mission by this engagement. The concept of 'deep literacy' advocated by Freire (1972) in which marginal communities come not just to the ability of reading and writing, but to the possibility of comprehending the forces which shape their lives, translates in the context of urban mission as the process by which the disadvantaged themselves preach the gospel in their own communities (Rhodes, 1996), and that such stories are likely 'to be the trigger for the transforming of those who put themselves in the position of caring' (Morisy, 1997: 6). In this way, parishes like St Aubyn's are not the recipients of others' missionary activity, but discover their own indigenous and unique path; furthermore, the church itself (especially those living in entitlement) is likely to be re-equipped and transformed by the stories of the poor if ecclesial structures allow them the time and space to be heard.

Finally, we might ask about the long-term lessons from this interaction, and given sharply changed economic circumstances compared to the start of the regeneration programme (2001), what the parish's future planning might include. One of the successes of this particular NDC (New Deals for Communities) project has been working as a partnership between residents, statutory agencies and appointed, special-interest members. The role of the local church as a credible partner, perceived somewhere between a community group and a voluntary agency, must not be wasted in planning the succession to the Community Partnership. Personally, I have expressed with others the sense of loss which 2011 will bring in terms of contacts, support and community working. We probably cannot, and I would not wish to, go back to a strategy of ecclesial isolation. One lesson, however, is that the Church's involvement is almost never neutral, but that advantages as well as disadvantages cannot be known in advance.

The most visible evidence of economic difficulty has been the slowdown of private sector new building, especially in the reclaimed naval estate where housing, a shopping centre and other commercial premises are envisaged. It is much too early to say whether the problems usually associated with poverty and deprivation will return to Devonport, notwithstanding the development outlined here. What is apparent now, however, is that over the ten years of the Community Partnership many people have been given a voice for the first time in local decision-making, and others have sharpened and focused the voices they already had. Even those who have loudly contested decisions can be counted a partial success in this respect. A mini Local Strategic Partnership is in embryonic form, as well as a couple of Community Trusts, and it is hoped that the spirit of partnership working will continue through these bodies. The role of the parish at this level may be threefold: to encourage and support engaged residents to continue and bring others with them; to prevent a return to community groups competing for limited funding; and to ensure that large statutory and voluntary agencies honour their commitment to work alongside local residents, and work with one another. In other words, telling stories of hope for the future, which link Freirean concepts of literacy with the missionary promise of the kingdom.

St Philip's Church and Centre, Leicester: Presence and Engagement

MANDY FORD

Widely reported to be on track to become Britain's first 'plural city',[1] Leicester is undoubtedly one of the most diverse cities in Britain. Waves of migration, beginning with the arrival of Afro-Caribbean people in the post-war period, Asian families expelled from Uganda in the 1970s, people from Montserrat fleeing the devastation of volcanic eruption on the island in the 1980s, Somali refugees in the 1990s, and most recently young Eastern Europeans looking for work, have contributed to the variety of population groups in the city. The city's faith communities include significant groups of Christians, Hindus, Muslims and Sikhs, together with the largest concentration of Jains outside London.[2]

In the aftermath of the Oldham, Burnley and Bradford disturbances in 2001 there was already anxiety in the air about the breakdown of civil society in areas of ethnic diversity. Leicester was held up as an example of a city with positive relations between communities, probably due mainly to the existence of many different groups, rather than a binary split in the population. The importance of good relationships between faith communities on the ground and faith leaders became a political as well as social necessity, which would be brought to crisis point by the events in the United States on 11 September later in that same year.

The Church of England had set up a task group to consider the state of interfaith relations which delivered its findings in a report to Synod, *Presence and Engagement*, in July 2005. The paper considered the place of the Church of England in areas where there was significant representation of other faiths. Among the twenty parishes in the country with the highest proportion of other faiths, three were in Leicester: of these, two were the neighbouring parishes of Evington and St Philip's.[3]

This was the beginning of a conscious exploration of what it means to live as Christians, and in particular to be the Anglican parish church, in an area where many neighbours are committed to another faith. For the people of St Philip's it meant exploring and examining their past as well as facing the reality of the present and searching for new and different possibilities in the future. Among the recommendations of the report was that centres should be set up to help the wider Church to engage with the experience of churches in multi-faith areas, to inform interfaith dialogue and understanding and to equip clergy and others to work in such areas.

Rooting the vision

In the year 2000 Canon Dr Andrew Wingate, the Bishop of Leicester's Interfaith Adviser, was appointed Associate Priest of St Philip's. Andrew was widely known, respected and well liked by many leaders in Muslim, Hindu and Sikh communities. He has a gift for friendship and an openness to others, as well as an astute theological mind. He played a significant part in setting up the St Philip's Centre for Study and Engagement in a Multi-Faith Society. The parish were persuaded to invest resources from their reserves into the Centre and to provide not only meeting spaces in the church, but also the former vicarage to provide offices, meeting rooms and accommodation for students.

The vision of the Centre is 'for a centre rooted in the multi faith context of Leicester, which will assist in equipping churches for ministry, service and mission in such a context'. Its mission: 'To enable Christians and churches to be a positive presence in a multi faith world, prepared to share their faith, to learn from other faiths, and to assist all in promoting the common good.'[4]

The Centre was opened by the Archbishop of Canterbury in 2006 and offers a range of opportunities for students from near and far to experience the varied faith communities of Leicester, to learn about other faiths, to learn to speak of their own faith confidently and to engage in dialogue. The Centre provides religious literacy training for a variety of public service providers and has particularly strong links with the churches of northern Europe. This is the 'public' face of St

Philip's, work which continues under the current incumbent, also an interfaith specialist, Canon Dr Alan Race, who organizes the Centre's links with the universities in the city.

Deep-rooted presence

What of the ordinary members of the church community? How do they experience their faith and make sense of their situation? What is their understanding of 'presence and engagement'? Significantly, alongside Canon Wingate's work in the Centre, the church was served by a vicar with considerable pastoral skills, Revd Diane Johnson. Diane worked hard to build up the confidence of an ageing congregation and to help them to understand the vision which the centre represented. Diane was also able to work with Muslim women in the area and so to widen the sphere of dialogue.

A recent study day with the congregation revealed a quiet and a growing sense of their role as a parish church alongside St Philip's Centre.[5] The congregation take pride in the work of the Centre, but they know that it is not a substitute for their own mission, and they are beginning to reflect on what mission might mean at a congregational rather than an institutional level. Significantly, there is a number of church members who are deeply rooted in the geographical area and whose stories are reflected in the local architecture. St Philip's, a handsome red-brick Arts and Crafts style church, was consecrated in 1913. It sits in the middle of an area of brick terraces and larger villas mainly built at the beginning of the twentieth century, with further expansion in the immediate post-war period. Some church members moved into the area as newly-weds in the 1950s. They look back on a period when the community was close knit, people walked to the local shops or took their children to school along the same streets, and there was a wide variety of clubs and social activities, many of which were centred on the church. The church was a thriving and significant part of the community, with a huge choir and Sunday school – in the years immediately after the war there were 22 Sunday school teachers and over 300 children. The church had a strong musical tradition and a great choir, sufficiently admired to be broadcast by the BBC on more than one occasion.

The effects of suburban flight and inward migration can be

imagined, but were probably initially slow enough not to impact on the original residents of the area, although church attendance inevitably dwindled throughout the 1970s and 1980s. When the church was badly damaged by a fire in 1996, it clearly no longer needed to accommodate the thousand or so for whom it was designed, and it was decided to take the opportunity to split the nave in half and create a new community space.

The most significant physical change in the area came the following year when the local Muslim community were granted planning permission for a new mosque. The mosque, the Masjid Umar, now stands directly opposite the church. It is a huge building with a central hall accommodating over 400 worshippers and ten further side rooms for prayer and study. At night floodlights illuminate the four minarets and a beautiful hemispherical dome rises above the building. Driving down the Evington Road on a Friday night, the streets are filled with families going to worship, the children to madrassa (Qur'an school), the men and women to prayer. Cars are parked on every pavement and the air is filled with noise and excitement. The building of the mosque has encouraged devout Muslims to move to the area so as to be able to attend daily prayer. The demographic has changed rapidly and the local population is almost certainly well over 80 per cent Muslim.

. . . and engagement?

It is inevitable that the long-term residents feel a sense of loss and at times feel overwhelmed by a culture which is not their own. When the mosque opened, in the same year as the reordered church, it was a visible sign which demonstrated how the area had changed – the physical structure consolidated what they had previously known only theoretically or notionally. However, their theology is principally incarnational, there is a sense that God is at work around them, and that they are able to flourish where they are and as they are. Church members speak with affection for local Muslim leaders they have come to know and are happy when Muslim, Sikh and Hindu neighbours attend significant events in the life of the church, as well as joint fundraising events – each year a Christian–Muslim dinner is held to raise funds for a Christian and a Muslim charity, usually to support those in need overseas. The community space in the church is used by a wide variety of groups, including a playgroup which is used by local children.

The concept of 'presence and engagement' seems to articulate a reason for staying in a place where the church might very easily feel a sense of failure. In recent years the church has revived its musical tradition, holding a number of high quality concerts. Students and families of young professionals have begun to move into the area and are gently refreshing the demographic of the church. Most significantly, when asked to dream about the future of their church, members spoke of a place of hospitality, where people of all faiths and none might experience a welcome, healing, sustenance and a listening ear. Encounters with neighbours of other faiths seem to have helped these Christians to be more articulate about their own faith. They have a clear sense of the difference between faith and culture, and a strong social gospel. They are not, it seems, interested in converting their neighbours, but rather in showing the love of Christ through their generosity of heart. Meanwhile the leadership of the church expresses the desire that a certain subtlety and excellence of interfaith relations might also continue to develop, from which the whole church could benefit.

The question arises as to whether the change has come quickly enough for this community to remain sustainable and whether the wider Church is prepared to support such communities should they cease to be able to sustain themselves.

Notes

Chapter 2
1 www.citylinks.org.uk.
2 www.eden-network.org.
3 www.streetpastors.co.uk.
4 www.transformnewham.com.
5 www.lovesouthend.org.
6 Shaftesbury (now Livability) undertook the official evaluation of the *Soul in the City* initiative in 2004 in conjunction with the Evangelical Alliance. The report is available from Jill Clark at jclark@livability.org.uk.

Chapter 4
1 Dual city is the language used by Manual Castells, the Spanish sociologist – see Mollenkopf & Castells 1991.
2 Clare Watkins discusses this in an article on the relationship between evangelization and renewal. 'Suggestions for a Critical and Constructive Account of the Relation of Church Renewal and the Mission to Evangelise', 2005, found at www.margaretbeaufort.cam.ac.uk/research/papers.
3 See www.umtp.org (click on the link to St Martin's).

Chapter 6
1 Royal Commission on Environmental Pollution, report published 6 March 2007.
2 Labour Party Manifesto 1997.
3 This is a phrase found frequently in Alison's writing, but see particularly Alison 2001.

Chapter 7
1 The inseparability of the person and the social order: based on diagram 2-5 in Myers 1999: 48.
2 The fourfold definition is taken from Atkinson et al. 1995: 28.

Chapter 8

1   It was apparent that the Unit's title showed little understanding of approaches to Social Exclusion based on relativity, agency and dynamics. (See for example Alcock, *Understanding Poverty*, 2006.)

2   See for example USPG's *The Christ We Share* (http://shop.uspg.org.uk/acatalog/Resource_packs_and_CDs.html) Or the exercise in Griffin and Powell 2009: 44.

Chapter 10

1   A fully inclusive 'open table' is practised in the Episcopal Church of St Gregory of Nyssen, the theological rationale is described in Fabian 2002.

2   For a discussion of open communion and its implications for our daily hospitality see Episcopal Church of the United States Theology Committee House of Bishops, 'Reflections on Holy Baptism and the Holy Eucharist' (2009).

Case Study 1

1   http://www.santegidio.org/EN/.

Case Study 4

1   BBC News, 11 September 2007, citing research from the University of Birmingham stated that Leicester would have a white minority by 2019, although no other ethnic group would have an overall majority. See http://news.bbc.co.uk/1/hi/england/leicestershire/6988815.stm. The research was later published in Nissa Finney and Ludi Simpson, *Sleepwalking to Segregation: Challenging Myths about Race and Migration* (London: Policy Press, 2009) from which it is clear that the authors do not accept the validity of the claim made on their behalf, but are challenging the entire premise.

2   The 2001 Census gives the following breakdown: Christians 45%, Hindus 15%, Muslim 11% and Sikh 4%. Source http://www.leicester.gov.uk/index.asp?pgid=1009#Rel.

3   Evington: Christian 10%, Hindu 23%, Muslim 49%, Sikh 7%. St Philip's: Christian 16%, Hindu 25%, Muslim 34%, Sikh 13%. Cited *Presence and Engagement*, p. 29

4   Cited in *St Philip's Church, Leicester: An Illustrated History*, a booklet produced for the 80th anniversary of the church in 2009.

5   Parish Engagement Day, 21 February 2009.

Bibliography

Abraham, William J. (1996) *The Logic of Evangelism*, Eerdmanns.

Alcock, Pete (2006) *Understanding Poverty*, third edition, Palgrave.

Alison, James (1994) *Knowing Jesus*, SPCK.

—— (2001) *Faith Beyond Resentment: Fragments Catholic and Gay*, Darton, Longman and Todd.

Atherton, John (2000) *Public Theology for Changing Times*, SPCK.

Atkinson, David et al. (1995) *Dictionary of Christian Ethics and Pastoral Theology*, IVP.

Avis, Paul (2005) *A Ministry Shaped by Mission*, T & T Clark.

Banawiratma, Johannes (2005) 'The Pastoral Cycle as Spirituality' in Frans Wijsen, Peter Henriot and Rodrigo Mejía (eds), *The Pastoral Cycle Revisited: A Critical Quest for Truth and Transformation*, Orbis.

Beckford, Robert (2004) *God and the Gangs: An Urban Toolkit for Those Who Won't Be Bought Out, Sold Out or Scared Out*, Darton, Longman and Todd.

Bedford, Nancy (2006) 'To Speak of God from More than One Place: Theological Reflections from the Experience of Migration' in Ivan Petrella (ed.), *Latin American Liberation Theology: The Next Generation*, Orbis.

Billings, Alan (2004) *Secular Lives, Sacred Hearts: The Role of the Church in a Time of No Religion*, SPCK.

Bosch, David J. (2008) 'Evangelism: Theological Currents and Cross-Currents Today' in Paul W. Chilcote and Laceye C. Warner (eds), *The Study of Evangelism: Exploring a Missional Practice of the Church*, Eerdmans.

Bowen, John P. (2009) 'What Happened Next? Vincent Donovan, Thirty Five Years On', *International Bulletin of Missionary Research*, Vol. 33, No. 2.

Brenner, Neil (2009) 'What is Critical Urban Theory' in *CITY* 13/2–3 June–September.

Brewin, Kester (2004) *The Complex Christ: Signs of Emergence in the Urban Church*, SPCK.

Brueggemann, Walter (2002) *The Land – Place as Gift, Promise and Challenge in Biblical Faith*, second edition, Fortress Press.

—— (2006) *Mandate to Difference*, Westminster John Knox Press.

147

Carey, George (2000) 'Evangelism' in Adrian Hastings (ed.), *The Oxford Companion to Christian Thought*, Oxford University Press.

Cartwright, Michael G. (2004) 'Witness' in Stanley Hauerwas and Samuel Wells (eds), *The Blackwell Companion to Christian Ethics*, Blackwell Publishing.

Cities: A Methodist Report (1997) NCH.

Codina, Victor (1993) 'Sacraments' in Ignacio Ellacuría and Jon Sobrino (eds), *Mysterium Liberationis. Fundamental Concepts of Liberation Theology*, Orbis.

Connolly, James and Steil, Justin (2009) 'Finding Justice in City' in Peter Marcuse, James Connolly, Johannes Novy, Ingrid Olivo, Cuz Potter, Justin Steil (eds), *Searching for the Just City Debates in Urban Theory and Practice*, Routledge.

Costas, Orlando (1989) *Liberating News! A Theology of Contextual Evangelization*, Eerdmans.

Cox, Stephen (2007) *'Faithful Cities'*: A Call For Celebration, Vision and Justice. A Fulcrum Review', http://www.fulcrumanglican.org.uk/news/2006/20061015cox.cfm?doc=146.

Davey, Andrew (2003) 'Flesh and Blood Cities', *Anvil* 20.2.

Davies, Oliver (2007) *Transforming Theology*, Continuum.

de Certeau, Michel (1988) 'Walking in the City' in *The Practice of Everyday Life*, University of California Press.

Dinham, Adam (2009) *Faiths, Public Policy and Civil Society: Problems, Policies, Controversies*, Palgrave Macmillan.

Donovan, Vincent (1982) *Christianity Rediscovered: An Epistle from the Masai*, SCM Press.

Dunn-Wilson, David (2005) *A Mirror for the Church: Preaching in the First Five Centuries*, Eerdmans.

Ekblad, Bob (2005) *Reading with the Damned*, Westminster John Knox Press.

Erskine, Chris (2003) *Concentric Church*, The Shaftesbury Society.

Fabian, Richard (2002) 'First the Table, then the Font', San Francisco, at www.saintgregorys.org/Resources_pdfs/FirsttheTable.pdf

Faith in the City (1985) *A Call to Church and Nation*, Archbishop of Canterbury's Commission on Urban Priority Areas, Church House Publishing.

Faithful Cities (2006) *A Call for Celebration: Vision and Justice*, Commission on Urban Life and Faith, Methodist Publishing.

Ford, David (1989) 'Faith in the Cities. Corinth and the Modern City' in Colin Gunton and Daniel Hardy (eds), *On Being the Church*, T&T Clark.

Ford, David and McFadyen, Al (1995) 'Praise' in Sedgwick (1995).

Freire, Paulo (1972) *Pedagogy of the Oppressed*, Penguin.

Furbey, Rob et al. (2006) *Faith as Social Capital*, Policy Press.

Gibson, Katherine (1994) *Postmodern Cities and Space*, Blackwell.

Girard, Rene (2000) *I see Satan Fall Like Lightning*, Orbis.

Glasson, Barbara (2006) *I Am Somewhere Else*, Darton, Longman and Todd.

Goddard, Giles (2008) 'Space for Grace', *Creating Inclusive Churches*, Canterbury Press.

Gorringe, Timothy J. (2002) *A Theology of the Built Environment: Justice, Empow-*

erment, Redemption, Cambridge University Press.

Graham, Elaine and Lowe, Stephen (2009) *What Makes a Good City?*, Darton, Longman and Todd.

Green, Laurie (1995) 'The Body: Physicality in the UPA' in Sedgwick (1995).

Griffin, Brad M. and Powell, Kara (2009) *Deep Justice Journeys Leader's Guide: 50+ Activities to Move from Mission Trips to Missional Living*, ZonderKidz.

Hardy, Daniel (2001) *Finding the Church*, SCM Press.

Hasler, Joe (2006) *Crying Out for a Polycentric Church: Christ Centred and Culturally Focussed Congregations*, Church in Society.

Haynes, John (2006) *Sub-merge. Living Deep in a Shallow World*, Regal.

The Hind Report (2003) *Formation for Ministry in a Learning Church. The Structure and Funding of Ordination Training*, General Synod paper, http://cofe.anglican.org/lifeevents/ministry/workofmindiv/tetc/safwp/sfot/sf ot_30.04.03.doc.

Holtam, Nicholas (2007) 'The Touchstones of Good Religion' in *Contact: Practical Theology and Pastoral Care*, 152.

Hsu, Albert Y. (2006) *The Suburban Christian. Finding Spiritual Vitality in the Land of Plenty*, IVP.

Hull, John (2006) *Mission Shaped Church: A Theological Response*, SCM.

Jeremias, Joachim (1975) *New Testament Theology*, SCM.

Kane, Margaret (1985) *What Kind of God?*, SCM.

Keith, Michael (2003) 'Cosmopolitanism and the Multicultural City', Charles Darwin 2003 Symposium, http://www.cdu.edu.au/cdss2003/presentations/symposium4/mkeithalice%20springs.doc.

Kilpin, Juliet and Murray, Stuart (2007) *Church Planting in the Inner City. The Urban Expression Story*, Grove Books.

Kim, Yung Suk (2009) *Christ's Body in Corinth*, Eerdmanns.

King, Martin Luther (1963) 'Pilgrimage to Non-Violence' in *Strength to Love*, Fount.

Lake, Frank (1986) *Clinical Theology*, Darton, Longman and Todd.

Latham, Steve (2007) *Some Issues in Urban Theology*, London Urban Theology Project – Private circulation.

Layard, Richard (2005) *Happiness: Lessons from a New Science*, Penguin Books.

Linthicum, Bob (2004) *Transforming Power*, InterVarsity Press.

Marchant, Colin (2004) 'The Story of Urban Mission in the UK' in Eastman, Michael and Latham, Steve (eds), *Urban Church, A Practitioners' Resource Book*, SPCK.

Marcuse, Peter (1995) 'Not Chaos, but Walls: Postmodernism and the Partitioned City' in Watson, Sophie and Gibson, Katherine, *Postmodern Cities and Space*, Blackwell.

Martin, David (2006) *The Breaking of the Image: Sociology of Christian Theory and Practice*, Regent College Publishing.

Massey, Doreen (2007) *World City*, Polity.

McIntosh, Mark A. (1998) *Mystical Theology: The Integrity of Spirituality and Theology*, Blackwell.

150   *Bibliography*

Millard, W. (2004) 'Banned Words' in Rem Koolhaas (ed.), *Content*, Taschen.

Mission Shaped Church (2004) Working Group of the Council for Mission and Public Affairs, Church House Publishing.

Mollenkopf, John H. and Castells, Manuel eds. (1991) *Dual City: Restructuring New York*, Russell Sage Foundation.

Morisy, Ann (1997) *Beyond the Good Samaritan, Community, Ministry and Mission*. Mowbray.

Moxnes, Halvor (2004) *Putting Jesus in his place*. Westminster John Knox Press.

Myers, Bryant (1999) *Walking with the Poor*, Orbis/World Vision.

Myers, Ched (1994) *Who Will Roll Away The Stone?*, Orbis.

—— (2008)*Binding the Strong Man*, twentieth anniversary edition, Orbis.

Myers, Ched and Enns, Elaine (2009) *Ambassadors of Reconciliation: New Testament Reflections on Restorative Justice and Peacemaking*, v. 1, Orbis.

Northcott, Michael (ed.) (1998) *Urban Theology: A Reader*, Cassell.

Peterson, Eugene (2005) *Christ Plays in Ten Thousand Places: A Conversation in Spiritual Theology*, Hodder & Stoughton.

Pontifical Council for Justice and Peace (2004) *Compendium of the Social Doctrine of the Church*, Continuum.

Radcliffe, Timothy (2008) *Why Go to Church? The Drama of the Eucharist*, Continuum.

Ramsey, Michael (1956) *The Gospel and the Catholic Church*, SPCK.

Rasmussen, Larry (ed.) (1989) *Reinhold Niebuhr: Theologian of Public Life*, Collins.

Rhodes, David (1996) *Faith in Dark Places*, London: Triangle.

Root, John (1987) 'What Sort of Nation?' in David Newman (ed.), *Taking on Faith in the City*, Grove booklets.

Russell, Hilary (2002) 'Trust in the City: Reviving and Enriching Urban Areas through Effective Social Policy,' *Anvil* 20.2.

—— (2004) *Evaluation of Urban Mission and Theology Newcastle east Deanery*, at www.umtp.org.

Sainsbury, Roger and Holden, John (1987) 'What Sort of Theology?' in David Newman (ed.), *Taking on Faith in the City*, Grove booklets.

Samuel, Vinay (2006) *Transforming our Cultures – A Gospel Agenda*, available at www.wheaton.edu/HNGR/resources/vinay_samuel.html.

Schillebeeckx, Edward (1990) *Church: The Human Story of God*, SCM.

Schreiter, Robert (1996) *The New Catholicity*, Orbis.

Sedgwick, Peter (ed.) (1995) *God in the City, Essays from the Archbishop's Urban Theology Group*, Mowbray.

Sedmak, Clemens (2002) *Doing Local Theology*, Orbis.

Selby, Peter (1995) *Rescue: Jesus and Salvation Today*, SPCK.

Shakespeare, Steven and Rayment-Pickard, Hugh (2006) *The Inclusive God: Reclaiming Theology for an Inclusive Church*, Canterbury Press.

Shorter, Aylward (1991) *The Church in the African City*, Geoffrey Chapman.

Sider, Ronald J. (2008) 'Evangelism, Salvation and Social Justice: Definitions and Interrelationships' in Paul W. Chilcote and Laceye C. Warner (eds), *The Study of Evangelism: Exploring a Missional Practice of the Church*, Eerdmans.

Simone, AbdouMalik (2004) *For the City Yet to Come*, Duke University Press.

Slater, Tim (2009) 'Missing Marcuse. On Gentrification and displacement' in *CITY* Vol 13/2–3, June–September.

Smith, Christine M. (1996) 'Preaching as an Art of Resistance', in Christine C. Neuger (ed.), *The Arts of Ministry*, John Knox Press.

Snyder, Susanna (2007) 'The Dangers of "Doing Our Duty": Reflections on Churches Engaging with People Seeking Asylum in the UK', *Theology* CX (857) September.

Stringfellow, William (1994) *Keeper of the Word*, Bill Wiley Kellerman (ed.), Eerdmans.

Sugden, Christopher and Samuel, Vinay (eds) (1999) *Mission as Transformation*, Regnum.

Sweeney, Jim and Watkins, Clare (nd) 'Evangelisation and Renewal Research Project: Rediscovering the Theological Heart of the Matter', see www.margaretbeaufort.cam.ac.uk/research/papers.

Tablet (2009) 'Rapped in Prayer', *The Tablet*.

Tanner, Kathryn (ed.) (2004) *Spirit in the Cities: Searching for Soul in the Urban Landscape*. Fortress.

Taylor, Michael (2002) *Poverty and Christianity*, SCM.

Theology Committee House of Bishops, Episcopal Church of the United States (2009) 'Reflections on Holy Baptism and the Holy Eucharist' at http://www.episcopalcafe.com/lead/theology/report_on_communing_the_u nbapt.html.

Tisdale, Leonora Tubbs (1997) *Preaching as Local Theology and Folk Art*, Fortress Press.

Torres-Fleming, Alexie (2009) 'Justice for the South Bronx,' *The Christian Century*, http://findarticles.com/p/articles/mi_m1058/is_15_126/ai_ n35579548/?tag=content;col1.

Vanhoozer, Kevin J., Anderson, Charles A. and Sleasman, Michael J. (2007) *Everyday Theology: How to Read Cultural Texts and Interpret Trends*, Baker Academic.

Villafañe, Eldin (2006) *Beyond Cheap Grace*, Eerdmans.

Vincent, John (1982) *Into the City*, Epworth.

Wainwright, Martin (2007) 'Hunt for Best or Worst Wayside Pulpit Puns', *Guardian*, Friday 16 March.

Wallis, Jim (1976) *Agenda for Biblical People*, Harper & Row.

Ward, Graham (2000) *Cities of God*, Routledge.

Watkins, Clare (2005) 'Suggestions for a Critical and Constructive Account of the Relation of Church Renewal and the Mission to Evangelise', found at www.margaretbeaufort.cam.ac.uk/research/papers.

Wilkinson, Richard G. (2005) *The Impact of Inequality: How to Make Sick Societies Healthier*, Routledge.

Wilkinson, Richard G. and Kate Pickett (2009) *The Spirit Level: Why More Equal Societies Almost Always Do Better*, Allen Lane.

Williams, Rowan (2002) Richard Dimbleby Lecture 2002, Thursday 19 December. www.archbishopofcanterbury.org/846.

Wright, Tom (2006) *Simply Christian*, SPCK.

Bible References

Author Index

Subject Index